The Beats

The Beats
A Graphic History

Text by Harvey Pekar et al.

Art by Ed Piskor et al.

Edited by Paul Buhle

A Novel Graphic from Hill and Wang

A division of Farrar, Straus and Giroux

New York

Hill and Wang
A division of Farrar, Straus and Giroux
18 West 18th Street, New York 10011

Grateful acknowledgement is made for permission to reprint lyrics from the following: "Lord of the Trenches," by Edward Sanders, PCC Music, BMI. "CIA Man," by Tuli Kupferberg, PCC Music, BMI. "Hallucination Horrors," by Tuli Kupferberg, Heavy Metal Music, BMI. "I Couldn't Get High," by Ken Weaver, Heavy Metal Music, BMI. "Slum Goddess," by Ken Weaver, Heavy Metal Music, BMI. "Doin' All Right," by Ted Berrigan, Heavy Metal Music, BMI. "Exorcism of the Pentagon," by Ed Sanders, Heavy Metal Music, BMI.
Grateful acknowledgement is made for permission to reprint poetry by Kenneth Patchen, courtesy of UC Santa Cruz Special Collections, Kenneth Patchen Archive.

Library of Congress Cataloging-in-Publication Data

Pekar, Harvey.
    The beats : a graphic history / text by Harvey Pekar et al.; art by Ed Piskor et al.; edited by Paul Buhle.— 1st ed.
        p.   cm.
    ISBN-13: 978-0-8090-9496-7 (alk. paper)
    ISBN-10: 0-8090-9496-7 (alk. paper)
    1. Beat generation—Comic books, strips, etc.   I. Piskor, Ed.   II. Buhle, Paul, 1944–   III. Title.

PS228.B6 P45 2009
810.9'0054—dc22

                                                                                2008043350

Designed by Laura Dumm

www.fsgbooks.com

1   3   5   7   9   10   8   6   4   2

Contents

Introduction

There was never anything like them in American literature and American culture, and it is unlikely that there will ever be anything much like them again. The Beat Generation stood between the social collectivism of the Franklin D. Roosevelt years and the do-your-own-thingism of the 1960s, squarely (even while hating "squares") within the era of Cold War anxieties. Against compulsory conformism, the Beats offered wild sex, recreational drug use, determined uprootedness, and most important, experimental writing of all kinds.

Allen Ginsberg's *Howl and Other Poems,* to take a single case in point, set new legal precedents for freedom of print and restored the role of the poet to a public place of influence and relevance lost for generations in the United States. The Beats also introduced poetry and prose that sounded like jazz, literature embracing Eastern religions (above all, Buddhism), American Indian themes, homosexuality, draft resistance, and a whole range of previously unacceptable, almost unutterable ideas. The Beats would collectively fade soon enough, victims of their own lifestyles, but their influence would grow. The Sixties counterculture seemed, in some ways, to be made by them and for them.

This last view is surely an exaggeration, but one with meaning, and not only for an American audience. Allen Ginsberg was crowned King of May in Prague, anticipating a peaceful, blue-jeans-clad 1968 uprising against Russian occupation. Across parts of Latin America, Africa, and Asia as well as Europe, the Beat writers probably have had more resonance with poets, novelists, social rebels, and hipsters than in the United States. Their influence is by no means spent. Young people in particular seem to rediscover them constantly, now in greater numbers than ever before, thanks to the Web.

The Beats' ultimate "meaning" is and probably always will be elusive. In a famous 1957 essay, Norman Mailer—their most prestigious defender—argued eloquently for their collective importance. Writing at a time when the "courage to be individual" was being severely tested in locked-down America, Mailer argued on behalf of those who identified with outsiderness, who sought in words to capture what the overwhelming majority of fellow citizens couldn't see or didn't want to see. These men and women, he wrote, had a solemn political, cultural, and spiritual mission—to which we might add that the Beats, in accepting no outside logic, whether capitalist, socialist, or any other, renewed the thrill of discovery on their own terms. They thereby invented a different model for the rebel artist/intellectual, and through their lives as well as their work, spoke to the questings of a new generation.

Another point is yet more elusive: the Beat role within the mass media culture of the 1950s and '60s. The writer and poet Diane di Prima reflected, later, that the Beats had been made up of little groups, insular and protective of their semi-hiddenness, thinking of themselves as a few hundred souls in a vast and hostile consumerist society. Then came the publicity splash, including the very coining of the word "Beatnik" by the sympathetic San Francisco newspaper columnist Herb Caen, in 1957. The "Beatnik" narrative suddenly blossomed into the gag theme of the year. Ernie Kovaks appeared on television in a long-sleeved striped T-shirt, wearing a beret and pounding on bongo drums, uttering inexplicable phrases. "Rent a Beatnik" parties and a "Beatnik for President" campaign (in 1960) captured the downbeat flavor of the cultural exit from the 1950s into the 1960s.

The book before you is a comic art production with no pretension to the depth of coverage and literary interpretation presented by hundreds of scholarly books in many languages, a literature also constantly growing. It has a different virtue, curiously in line, somehow, with the original vernacular popularization of the Beats.

Our artists, working from their own scripts or those provided by others, offer a visual and narrative interpretation that is fresh and insightful in its own right. The major scriptwriter, Harvey Pekar, and the editor, Paul Buhle, have worked together throughout the process, toiling over core issues and personalities. Ed Piskor, an artist far too young to have lived through the Beat saga but who is emphatically part of its legacies, has done the majority of the art. Other artists, including some of the best of several generations still working, and writers (including the central figure of City Lights Books, these past thirty years) have added their own efforts to capture the lasting wonder of the Beat Generation. No one claims this treatment to be definitive. But it is new, and it is vital.

—Paul Buhle and Harvey Pekar

THE BEATS:
KEROUAC, GINSBERG, AND BURROUGHS

STORY BY: **HARVEY PEKAR**   ART BY: **ED PISKOR**

JACK KEROUAC

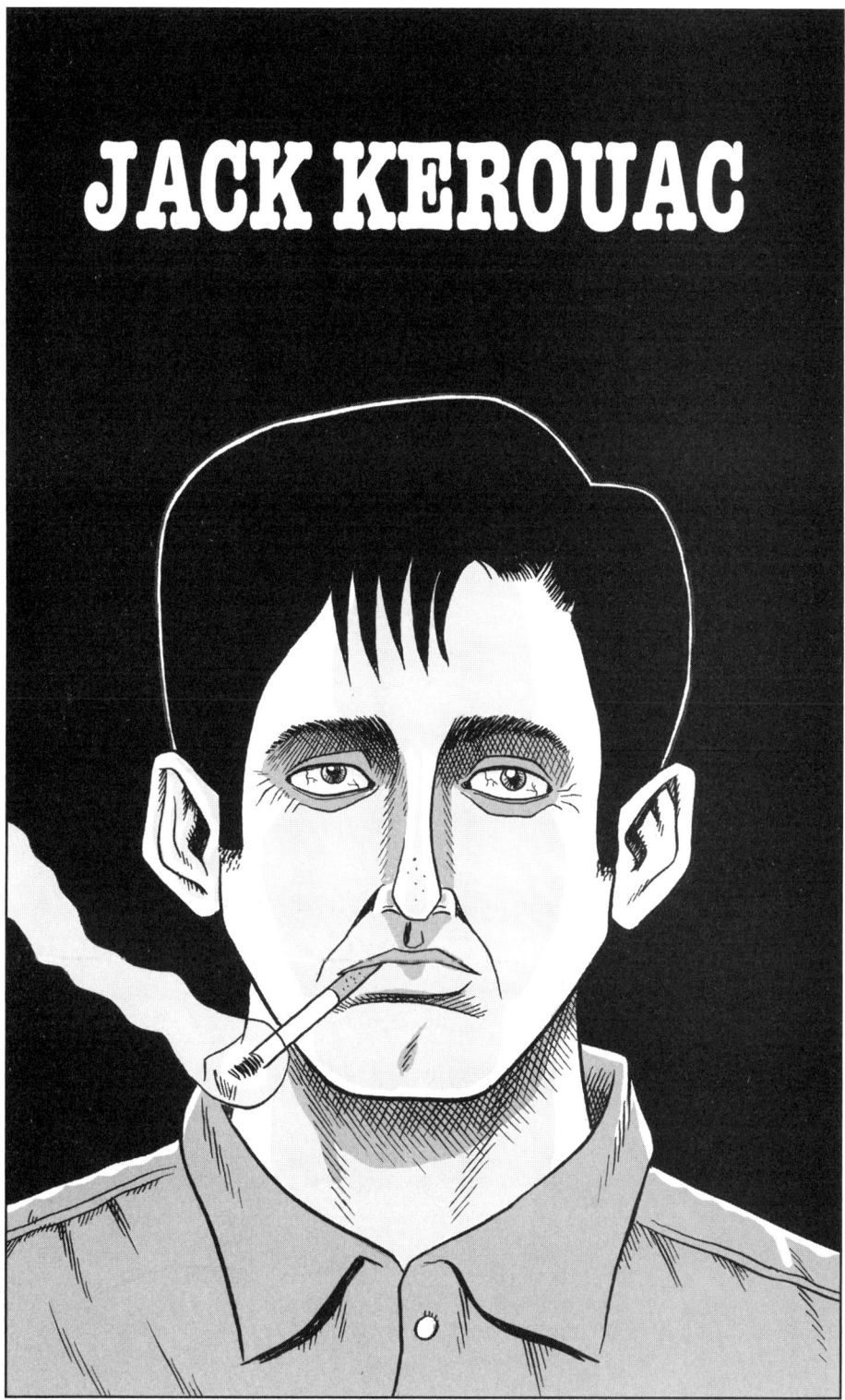

IN SEPTEMBER 1939, JACK KEROUAC MOVED TO NEW YORK FROM LOWELL, MASSACHUSETTS.

THE SON OF FRENCH CANADIAN PARENTS, HE WAS THERE THANKS TO A FOOTBALL SCHOLARSHIP HE'D RECEIVED AT COLUMBIA UNIVERSITY. BEFORE HE COULD ENTER COLUMBIA, HOWEVER, HE HAD TO MAKE UP SOME HIGH SCHOOL CREDITS AT HORACE MANN PREP SCHOOL.

HE STARRED ON HORACE MANN'S FOOTBALL TEAM BUT ALSO HAD FICTION PUBLISHED IN THE "HORACE MANN QUARTERLY." HE DEVELOPED A LOVE FOR LITERATURE AND WANTED TO BECOME A PROFESSIONAL WRITER.

AMONG HIS EARLY INFLUENCES WAS THE NOVELIST THOMAS WOLFE. JACK WAS AN AUTODIDACT WHO HAD READ ASSIDUOUSLY SINCE HIGH SCHOOL.

THOUGH KEROUAC GOT GOOD GRADES AT HORACE MANN AND COMPLETED HIS CREDITS, HE WAS ABSENT FROM CLASS OFTEN, CHECKING OUT THE JUNKIES AND PROSTITUTES IN TIMES SQUARE.

HEY, HOW MUCH YOU CHARGE?

HE QUICKLY BECAME A JAZZ FAN, AND ATTENDED THE LEGENDARY UPTOWN JAM SESSIONS AT WHICH CHARLIE PARKER, DIZZY GILLESPIE, AND THELONIOUS MONK AND OTHERS BEGAN INVENTING BEBOP.

YEAH, MAN, GO !!!

THE LONG MUSIC PHRASES OF THE BOPPERS HAD AN INFLUENCE ON KEROUAC'S PROSE.

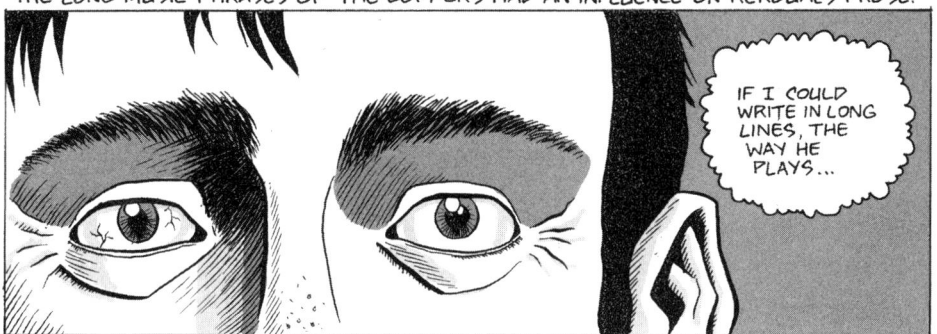

IF I COULD WRITE IN LONG LINES, THE WAY HE PLAYS...

DURING HIS FIRST YEAR ON COLUMBIA'S FOOTBALL TEAM, KEROUAC SUFFERED A BROKEN LEG AND HAD TO SIT OUT THE REST OF THE YEAR.

DAMMIT!

HE ALSO MET HIS FUTURE FIRST WIFE, EDIE PARKER, WHO WAS GOING TO BARNARD COLLEGE.

I'M SUPPOSED TO BE STUDYING ART BUT I'M NOT OPPOSED TO HAVING A GOOD TIME TOO.

IN FEBRUARY 1941 HE WROTE TO A FRIEND:

I No longer bother to study!!

yours Jack

BRIGHT, ATHLETIC, AND GOOD-LOOKING, KEROUAC WAS A POPULAR GUY, AND WAS VOTED VICE PRESIDENT OF THE SOPHOMORE CLASS, 1941-42 ACADEMIC YEAR.

WOW, THIS SURE BEATS HIGH SCHOOL.

ALREADY HE WAS DRINKING HEAVILY. HE STRUGGLED WITH AN ALCOHOL ADDICTION THROUGHOUT HIS LIFE.

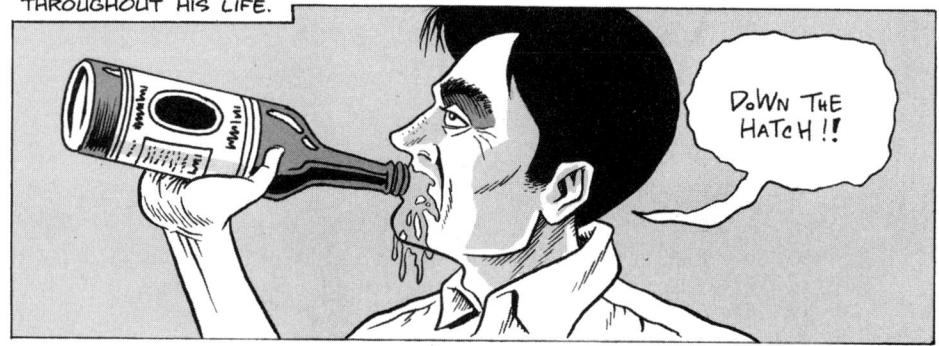

DoWN THE HATCH!!

KEROUAC KEPT UP A LIVELY RELATIONSHIP WITH MEN, TOO. HE WAS PROBABLY BISEXUAL, EVEN THOUGH HE WOULD NEVER ADMIT IT.

WHEN THE NEXT FOOTBALL SEASON ROLLED AROUND, THE COACH SAID KEROUAC WAS TOO SLOW TO START GAMES. HE WALKED OFF THE FIELD AND QUIT COLLEGE THE NEXT DAY.

WITH NO CLEAR PLAN OF HOW TO PROCEED, KEROUAC GOT A JOB AT A HARTFORD, CONNECTICUT, GAS STATION.

ON THANKSGIVING DAY KEROUAC MET WITH HIS BOYHOOD FRIEND, THE LOVE OF HIS EARLY LIFE, SAMMY SAMPAS, WHO WAS LATER KILLED DURING THE ALLIES' INVASION OF ANZIO. KEROUAC GREATLY ADMIRED SAMMY'S LEFT-LEANING POLITICS, WHICH KEROUAC LATER ABANDONED AND RENOUNCED, AND SAMMY'S SPIRITUALITY, WHICH HELPED KEEP KEROUAC TOGETHER.

YOU AND I ALONE IN THIS ROOM.

AFTER THE GAS STATION JOB KEROUAC WENT BACK TO HIS FAMILY AND WORKED A FEW JOBS AROUND LOWELL.

EVENTUALLY HE RETURNED TO NEW YORK BEFORE GOING ON TO WASHINGTON, D.C., WHERE HE HAD A CONSTRUCTION JOB ON THE PENTAGON.

THEN KEROUAC JOINED THE NATIONAL MARITIME UNION AND SHIPPED OUT WITH THE MERCHANT MARINE TO GREENLAND.

WASHING POTS AND PANS ISN'T MY IDEA OF FUN, BUT I'M LEARNING, GETTING MORE EXPERIENCE.

WHILE AT SEA HE CONCEIVED OF A NOVEL, "THE SEA IS MY BROTHER," WHICH HE COMPLETED LATER IN ROUGH FORM. IT HAS SO FAR NEVER BEEN PUBLISHED, THOUGH KEROUAC DESCRIBED IT AS "AN IMMENSE SAGA."

ON HIS RETURN TO NEW YORK HE WENT BACK TO COLUMBIA AND FOOTBALL, BUT HAD A FALLING OUT WITH COACH LOU LITTLE AND QUIT THE TEAM AGAIN.

THIS TIME I'M NOT COMING BACK !!!

HE THEN QUIT COLUMBIA FOR GOOD AND WENT BACK TO LOWELL.

HI, FOLKS, I'M HOME AGAIN!

THIS TIME HIS PLAN OF ACTION WAS TO TAKE THE NAVY TEST FOR OFFICERS SCHOOL AND, IF HE PASSED IT, RETURN TO COLLEGE ON THE V-12 PROGRAM.

9

KEROUAC FLUNKED THE TEST, BUT HE STILL JOINED THE NAVY, ONLY AT THE BOTTOM, NOT AS AN OFFICER.

HOW COULD I HAVE SCREWED UP SO BADLY?

AFTER A FEW WEEKS IN BOOT CAMP, KEROUAC WANTED TO GET OUT OF THE NAVY. HE ACCOMPLISHED THIS BY FEIGNING PSYCHOTIC BEHAVIOR.

WILL YOU OBEY THAT ORDER?

I'D PREFER NOT TO.

SEE SHORT STORY "BARTLEBY THE SCRIVENER" BY HERMAN MELVILLE.

IN MAY 1943, KEROUAC WAS DISCHARGED FROM THE NAVY ON THE GROUNDS OF "INDIFFERENT CHARACTER." AT LEAST IT WASN'T DISHONORABLE.

GOOD, IT'S NOT DISHONORABLE.

MOM WILL BE GLAD.

THIS TIME WHEN KEROUAC WENT HOME IT WAS TO NEW YORK CITY, WHERE HIS PARENTS HAD MOVED.

IT'S ME.

KEROUAC SIGNED ON FOR A MERCHANT MARINE TRIP, THIS TIME HEADED FOR LIVERPOOL. HE WAS CONSIDERED A HERO FOR SPOTTING A GERMAN MINE.

AFTER RETURNING, HE LOOKED UP HIS OLD GIRLFRIEND EDIE PARKER, WHO WAS LIVING WITH WILLIAM BURROUGHS'S FUTURE MATE, JOAN VOLLMER, AND MOVED IN WITH THEM. THEY WERE HAPPY TO HAVE HIM. EDIE SUPPORTED JACK FINANCIALLY.

WHILE LIVING WITH EDIE, JACK MET SOME KEY MEMBERS OF THE FUTURE BEAT SCENE. THERE WAS COLUMBIA UNDER-GRADUATE LUCIEN CARR FROM ST. LOUIS. BRILLIANT BUT SOMETIMES CYNICAL, MEAN, AND SNOBBISH, CARR WAS NOT AN ASPIRING WRITER, THOUGH HE HAD A WAY WITH WORDS.

CARR WAS JOINED IN NEW YORK BY TWO ST. LOUIS ACQUAINTANCES, BURROUGHS AND DAVE KAMMERER.

THEN CARR MET ALLEN GINSBERG, ANOTHER COLUMBIA STUDENT, AND SOON KEROUAC KNEW EVERYONE.

KAMMERER, WHO WAS GAY, WAS OBSESSED WITH CARR AND STALKED HIM.

ONE NIGHT THE TWO GOT INTO A DRUNKEN ARGUMENT IN A BAR, WHICH CONTINUED WHEN THEY WENT TO RIVERSIDE PARK. CARR STABBED KAMMERER TO DEATH, WEIGHED HIM DOWN WITH STONES, AND DUMPED HIM IN THE HUDSON RIVER.

SCARED, HE WENT TO BURROUGHS TO ASK HIM WHAT HE SHOULD DO NEXT.

12

NEXT CARR GOT HOLD OF KEROUAC, WHO HELPED HIM DISPOSE OF SOME EVIDENCE.

THROW IT INTO THE SEWER.

CARR REAPPEARED IN COURT A COUPLE DAYS LATER WITH A LAWYER TO PLEAD SELF-DEFENSE. BUT HE WAS CHARGED WITH MURDER.

KEROUAC AND BURROUGHS WERE ARRESTED AS MATERIAL WITNESSES. KEROUAC, WHO DIDN'T HAVE THE MONEY TO MAKE BAIL, TURNED TO EDIE FOR IT.

I'LL GIVE IT TO YOU IF YOU MARRY ME.

UH... WELL, OK. I GUESS SO.

SO JACK GOT MARRIED, WENT BACK TO JAIL, AND THEN WAS BAILED OUT AND WENT TO DETROIT WITH EDIE.

C'MON, C'MON!

CARR MANAGED TO CONVINCE THE COURT HE'D KILLED KAMMERER IN SELF-DEFENSE (PRESUMABLY AFTER KAMMERER ATTACKED HIM SEXUALLY) AND ONLY HAD TO SERVE TWO YEARS FOR MANSLAUGHTER.

KEROUAC STAYED IN DETROIT A COUPLE OF MONTHS. EDIE SAID SHE CAUGHT HIM IN BED WITH HER GIRLFRIEND.

YOU LOUSY!!

NOW WAIT A MINUTE. I CAN EXPLAIN!

JACK WAS BACK IN NEW YORK IN OCTOBER 1944. THIS TIME HE HUNG OUT MORE WITH GINSBERG AND BURROUGHS.

BURROUGHS WAS REALLY LIVING A LOW LIFE THEN, STRUNG OUT ON DRUGS, FENCING STOLEN ITEMS.

HOW MUCH YOU WANT FOR THIS?

AROUND THIS TIME BURROUGHS INTRODUCED KEROUAC TO ONE OF HIS DISREPUTABLE FRIENDS, HERBERT HUNCKE, A THIEF, JUNKIE, CONMAN, AND HUSTLER. HUNCKE, THOUGH A BRIGHT GUY FROM A MIDDLE-CLASS BACKGROUND, HAD BEEN INTO THIS DISSOLUTE LIFE FOR YEARS. HE SERVED AS A SORT OF TOUR GUIDE FOR KEROUAC AND HIS FRIENDS. HE EVEN PUT JACK ON TO THE WORD "BEAT."

MAN, I'M BEAT!

"BEAT"... THAT COULD MEAN EXHAUSTED BUT IT'S ALSO CONNECTED WITH "BEATIFIC" AND "BEATITUDE."

KEROUAC WAS ALWAYS TRYING TO GET HIS FRIENDS TO WRITE. HE EVEN CONVINCED THE HARVARD EDUCATED BURROUGHS TO AUTHOR A BOOK OF FICTION WITH HIM, "AND THE HIPPOS WERE BOILED IN THEIR TANKS," A WORK OF HARD-BOILED FICTION A LA DASHIELL HAMMETT. THEY SENT IT TO VARIOUS PUBLISHING HOUSES BUT THE MANUSCRIPT WAS REJECTED BY ALL OF THEM.

I DON'T KNOW HOW I LET YOU TALK ME INTO WRITING THAT THING.

IN JANUARY 1945, JACK AND EDIE TRIED TO RECONCILE, AND RENTED A ROOM IN JOAN VOLLMER'S APARTMENT. VOLLMER WAS A BRILLIANT WOMAN WORKING HER WAY THROUGH SCHOOL.

SEEMS LIKE OLD TIMES.

THEN BURROUGHS MOVED INTO VOLLMER'S APARTMENT AND, SUPRISINGLY, BECAUSE HE'D ALWAYS BEEN A HOMOSEXUAL, THEY BECAME LOVERS.

YOU'RE SUPPOSED TO BE A FAGGOT BUT YOU'RE AS GOOD AS A PIMP IN BED.

BURROUGHS MARRIED VOLLMER IN 1945, BUT HE GOT HER SO INVOLVED IN DRUGS THAT SHE WAS CONTINUALLY WASTED, OFTEN ON SPEED.

MEANWHILE, KEROUAC AND GINSBERG GOT TOGETHER SEXUALLY. BUT KEROUAC, BISEXUAL IN PRACTICE, WAS ALSO HOMOPHOBIC.

THE BLOWEE IS HETEROSEXUAL. THE BLOWER IS HOMOSEXUAL.

KEROUAC GOT HOOKED ON SPEED TOO, AND HAD A HARD TIME SHAKING IT UNTIL THE 1950'S.

AT THIS TIME KEROUAC BECAME FRIENDS WITH HAL CHASE, AN EX-SOLDIER FROM COLORADO WHO ATTENDED COLUMBIA. CHASE AND ANOTHER COLORADOAN, ED WHITE, INTRODUCED KEROUAC TO THE SOON-TO-BE-LEGENDARY NEAL CASSADY.

'SUP.

HOW YA DOIN'?

IN DECEMBER 1946, CASSADY ARRIVED IN NEW YORK FROM DENVER WITH A SIXTEEN-YEAR-OLD WIFE. HE WAS TWENTY, A PRODUCT OF THE STREETS WHO'D BEEN IN JAIL MANY TIMES FOR VARIOUS CRIMES. HE WAS ALSO GOOD-LOOKING, WELL-BUILT, AND HAD AN INSATIABLE SEXUAL APPETITE THAT INCLUDED BOTH MEN AND WOMEN. A "NATURAL" MAN, HE BECAME KEROUAC'S IDOL.

CASSADY WAS TO BECOME KEROUAC'S MODEL FOR DEAN MORIARTY IN "ON THE ROAD." WRITING OF NEAL, HE SAID,

...THE ONLY PEOPLE FOR ME ARE THE MAD ONES, THE ONES WHO ARE MAD TO LIVE, MAD TO TALK, MAD TO BE SAVED, DESIROUS OF EVERYTHING AT THE SAME TIME, THE ONES WHO NEVER YAWN OR SAY A COMMONPLACE THING, BUT BURN, BURN, BURN LIKE FABULOUS YELLOW ROMAN CANDLES EXPLODING LIKE SPIDERS ACROSS THE STARS AND IN THE MIDDLE YOU SEE THE BLUE CENTER-LIGHT POP AND EVERY-BODY GOES "AWWW."

CASSADY WAS KEROUAC'S DREAM MAN. HE HAD TO HAVE SEX EVERY DAY AND ALSO MASTURBATED SEVERAL TIMES DAILY. HE WAS NEVER FAITHFUL TO HIS WIVES AND DIDN'T PRETEND TO BE. HE LOVED DRIVING FAST CARS AND BURNED, BURNED, BURNED.

CASSADY MOOCHED HIS WAY THROUGH HIS NEW YORK VISIT AS GINSBERG AND KEROUAC VIED FOR HIM SEXUALLY. BOTH PLANNED TO TRAVEL TO MEET HIM, AND EACH DID. THEY COMPETED FOR NEAL UNTIL HE WENT WEST AGAIN. BOTH PLANNED TO FOLLOW HIM. KEROUAC'S AND CASSADY'S LONG JOURNEYS TOGETHER WERE THE BASIS OF "ON THE ROAD."

WHEN CASSADY RETURNED TO DENVER, HE SENT KEROUAC AN UNINHIBITED, EXUBERANT LETTER THAT MADE JACK WANT TO WRITE LIKE CASSADY, FREE OF CONSTRAINT AND WITHOUT GOING BACK TO CHANGE ANYTHING. KEROUAC WOULD LATER CALL THIS FREE STYLE OF WRITING "SPONTANEOUS PROSE."

CAN'T STOP, CAN'T STOP OR I'LL LOSE MY GROOVE.

IN 1946 KEROUAC BEGAN WRITING A SEMIAUTOBIOGRAPHICAL NOVEL, "THE TOWN AND THE CITY," IN SOME WAYS IMPRESSIVE BUT NOT PARTICULARLY ORIGINAL. IT HAD A BIT OF AN ACADEMIC QUALITY.

IT TOOK JACK SEVERAL YEARS TO FINISH IT AND HE HAD A ROUGH TIME GETTING IT PRINTED. IT WAS FINALLY PUBLISHED IN 1950 TO GENERALLY FAVORABLE REVIEWS, BUT IT SOLD POORLY AND WAS QUICKLY FORGOTTEN.

IT'S ONLY BEEN OUT A FEW MONTHS AND IT'S STOPPED SELLING.

IN 1947 KEROUAC BUSSED AND HITCHHIKED HIS WAY TO DENVER TO VISIT NEAL. GINSBERG WAS ALREADY THERE, AS WELL AS CAROLYN ROBINSON, NEAL'S FUTURE WIFE.

HEY, NEAL, GOOD TO SEE YOU. WHO'S THE GIRL?

NEAL TRIED TO DIVIDE HIS TIME AMONG THEM, BUT SATISFIED NO ONE. SEEN ANOTHER WAY, THEY WERE A THREE-SOME, IN AN EXPERIMENT THAT WOULD BECOME MORE COMMON IN FUTURE GENERATIONS.

AFTER DENVER KEROUAC WENT TO SAN FRANCISCO, WHERE HE WORKED AS A SECURITY GUARD. HE BOASTED ABOUT...

... BEING A FULL-FLEDGED MEMBER OF THE SAUSALITO SECURITY FORCE.

LOBBY

CAFE

MEANWHILE, CASSADY AND GINSBERG VISITED BURROUGHS IN TEXAS, WHERE HE WAS GROWING MARIJUANA TO BE SOLD IN NEW YORK ON A 99-ACRE FARM.

BURROUGHS AND HIS WIFE LIVED IN FILTHY CONDITIONS.

HEY, ISN'T YOUR KID SHITTING IN THE REVEREWARE?

GINSBERG WENT TO HOUSTON TO SIGN UP FOR WORK ON A SHIP HEADED FOR DAKAR, SENEGAL.

I CAN'T GET ANYTHING GOING WITH NEAL, MAN. I FEEL DEPRESSED.

KEROUAC'S MONEY RAN OUT AT THIS POINT AND HE HITCHHIKED BACK TO NEW YORK TO MOVE IN WITH HIS MOM.

WELCOME BACK!

ON JULY 4 KEROUAC MET JOHN CLELLON HOLMES, WHO WOULD PUBLISH AN AUTO-BIOGRAPHICAL NOVEL, "GO," ABOUT THE BEAT SCENE. HE WAS THE FIRST TO USE THE TERM "BEAT GENERATION" IN PRINT, THOUGH HE FREELY ADMITTED HE'D GOTTEN IT FROM A CONVERSATION WITH KEROUAC.

"BEAT GENERATION."

WOW, THAT HAS A RING TO IT.

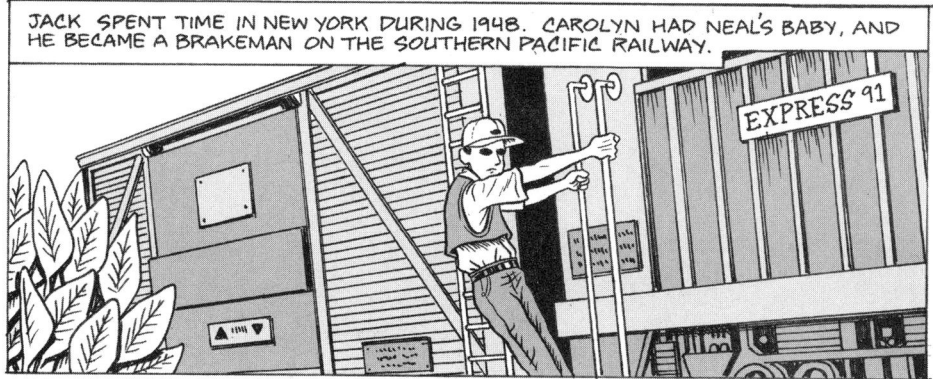

JACK SPENT TIME IN NEW YORK DURING 1948. CAROLYN HAD NEAL'S BABY, AND HE BECAME A BRAKEMAN ON THE SOUTHERN PACIFIC RAILWAY.

EXPRESS 91

LATER IN '48 JACK VISITED HIS SISTER, NIN, A COUPLE TIMES IN ROCKY MOUNT, NORTH CAROLINA. HE CONTINUED TO STAY CLOSE TO HIS FAMILY.

JACK RETURNED TO NEW YORK IN EARLY 1949 AND WORKED ON SOME NEW NOVELS WHILE TRYING TO SELL THE WOLFE-INFLUENCED "THE TOWN AND THE CITY" TO A PUBLISHER.

I'D LIKE TO SPEAK TO GIROUX, PLEASE.

FINALLY HE WAS ABLE TO SELL IT TO HARCOURT BRACE, AND IT WAS RELEASED IN 1950. KEROUAC WAS A HAPPY MAN.

HALLELUJAH !!!

WHILE "THE TOWN AND THE CITY" DIDN'T SELL WELL, IT HELPED GIVE KEROUAC THE IMPETUS TO WORK ON OTHER NOVELS.

I SHOULD TRY TO WRITE MORE ABOUT MY YEARS IN LOWELL.

21

ANOTHER 1950 OCCURRENCE WAS KEROUAC'S TRIP WITH CASSADY TO MEXICO CITY, WHERE BURROUGHS HAD BEEN LIVING SINCE HIS LAST DRUG BUST AND WORKING ON "JUNKIE," A CLASSIC OF ITS KIND, WHICH GINSBERG, WHO WAS ALWAYS ACTING AS AN UNPAID AGENT FOR OTHER WRITERS, ENCOURAGED HIM TO WRITE AND FINALLY GOT ACE BOOKS TO PUBLISH. HIS CONTACT AT ACE WAS CARL SOLOMON, WHO HAD BEEN IN A PSYCHIATRIC HOSPITAL WITH GINSBERG AND WHO WAS ONE OF THE INSPIRATIONS FOR "HOWL."

KEROUAC DIDN'T ACCOMPLISH MUCH IN MEXICO, BUT WHEN HE CAME BACK TO THE STATES HE STARTED WORK ON A SERIES OF BOOKS OF VARIOUS KINDS, WHICH HE WAS ABLE TO GET PUBLISHED ONLY AFTER "ON THE ROAD" WAS PRINTED.

BUT SOON KEROUAC'S MAIN FOCUS WAS GETTING "ON THE ROAD" WRITTEN AND PUBLISHED. THE BOOK WAS ABOUT HIS AND CASSADY'S HITCHHIKING ALL OVER THE COUNTRY AND WHAT THEY ENCOUNTERED. ITS REALISM WAS HEIGHTENED BY JACK'S "SKETCHING," WRITING DOWN IN A NOTEBOOK DIALOGUE AND ACTION HAPPENING AROUND HIM WHILE IT HAPPENED.

WHADDA YOU MEAN, YOU'RE BROKE?

HE INITIALLY TYPED "ON THE ROAD" ON A 120-FOOT-LONG PAPER ROLL, NOT WANTING TO STOP AND CHANGE PAPER WHILE HE WAS ON FIRE WITH IDEAS.

JACK GOT MARRIED AGAIN IN 1950 TO JOAN HAVERTY, WHO SUPPORTED HIM FOR A SHORT TIME BEFORE DUMPING HIM. SHE CLAIMED SHE HAD A BABY BY JACK, BUT COULDN'T PROVE IT IN COURT. SHE RELENTLESSLY LITIGATED FOR MONEY.

YOU'VE BEEN HAVING A FREE RIDE UP TO NOW, BUT JUST WAIT!

"SO THEN WE DIDN'T HAVE ANYWHERE TO DO IT SO I PUSHED HER AGAINST A GARAGE WALL..."

BOY, NEAL IS SOMETHING.

(A LETTER FROM CASSADY.)

JACK TOOK THE PAPER-ROLL VERSION OF "ON THE ROAD" TO ROBERT GIROUX, HIS EDITOR ON "THE TOWN AND THE CITY," BUT GIROUX WAS TAKEN ABACK BY IT.

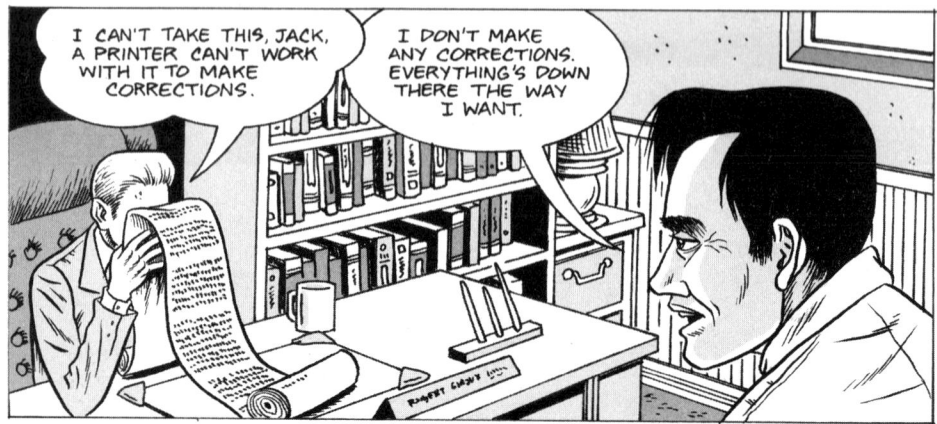

I CAN'T TAKE THIS, JACK, A PRINTER CAN'T WORK WITH IT TO MAKE CORRECTIONS.

I DON'T MAKE ANY CORRECTIONS. EVERYTHING'S DOWN THERE THE WAY I WANT.

IN MEXICO BURROUGHS AND JOAN, BOTH DRUNK, PLAYED A GAME OF "WILLIAM TELL" DURING WHICH BURROUGHS AIMED AT A GLASS ON HER HEAD, BUT SHOT HER IN THE FOREHEAD.

BY JANUARY 1952 HE WAS OUT OF PRISON, AND, PARTLY DUE TO MEXICO'S CORRUPT COURTS AND HIS FATHER'S MONEY, HE BEAT THE RAP.

AFTER THAT BURROUGHS TOOK OFF FOR TANGIER, WHERE NARCOTICS AND YOUNG BOYS WERE CHEAP.

24

IN NEW YORK KEROUAC TYPED "ON THE ROAD" CONVENTIONALLY AND GAVE IT TO AN AGENT TO SELL.

SEE WHAT YOU CAN DO WITH THIS.

WITHOUT A HOME OR A JOB, WHEN KEROUAC RECEIVED AN INVITATION FROM CASSADY TO GO TO SAN FRANCISCO, HE WENT.

AFTER A WHILE CASSADY GOT TIRED OF SUPPORTING JACK, WHO WAS SEXUALLY ENGAGED WITH HIS WIFE. KEROUAC EVENTUALLY WOUND UP WITH HIS MOTHER AND SISTER IN NORTH CAROLINA.

SURPRISE!

MOVING BETWEEN NEW YORK AND NORTH CAROLINA, KEROUAC TRIED UNSUCCESS-FULLY TO SELL "ON THE ROAD" AND A COUPLE OF OTHER NOVELS HE HAD FINISHED.

THIS IS MY BEST STUFF AND THOSE IDIOTS WON'T TOUCH IT. WHAT IDIOTS!! I'M THE JAMES JOYCE OF MY GENERATION.

25

IN 1952 JOHN CLELLON HOLMES PUBLISHED "GO," WHICH HAS SUBSEQUENTLY BEEN CALLED THE FIRST "BEAT" NOVEL, IN WHICH HE, GINSBERG, AND KEROUAC APPEAR THINLY DISGUISED. KEROUAC FELT UPSET BECAUSE HE WASN'T ABLE TO GET CREDIT FOR BEING FIRST.

OH NO, NOW THIS GUY, WHO CAN'T TOUCH MY WORK, HAS A NEW BOOK OUT.

KEROUAC TOOK REFUGE WITH THE CASSADYS IN SAN FRANCISCO, AND NEAL GOT JACK A BRAKEMAN'S JOB TOO.

TAKE IT EASY, JACK, YOU MIGHT SLIP.

IN NOVEMBER 1952, "THE NEW YORK TIMES MAGAZINE" PUBLISHED HOLMES'S ARTICLE "THIS IS THE BEAT GENERATION." HOLMES, HOWEVER, ALWAYS CREDITED JACK WITH INVENTING THAT LABEL, SO KEROUAC DIDN'T FEEL ENTIRELY UPSTAGED.

JACK SPENT THE CHRISTMAS 1952 HOLIDAYS WITH HIS MOTHER, WHO HAD MOVED BACK TO NEW YORK.

IN 1953 KEROUAC FINISHED "MAGGIE CASSIDY," AND BURROUGHS'S "JUNKIE" WAS PUBLISHED. BEAT LITERATURE WAS MAKING PROGRESS, BUT BOTH AUTHORS WOULD HAVE TO GO THROUGH A LOT MORE BEFORE BECOMING APPRECIATED.

ANOTHER STEP FORWARD WAS THAT "ON THE ROAD" WAS TAKEN ON BY THE HIGHLY REGARDED EDITOR MALCOLM COWLEY AT VIKING, THOUGH COWLEY WANTED JACK TO DO A GREAT DEAL OF REWRITING.

HOW ABOUT TAKING ON "DOCTOR SAX," TOO?

NOT UNLESS YOU REVISE AND SIMPLIFY IT.

THINKING HIMSELF AT A STANDSTILL, KEROUAC SHIPPED OUT ON A BOAT TO PANAMA.

MY JOB IS SHIT, BUT I DIG THE WOMEN AND THE WEATHER HERE.

IN AUGUST 1953, KEROUAC BECAME INVOLVED WITH A BEAUTIFUL BLACK WOMAN, ALENE LEE, AND THEY WERE TOGETHER FOR ABOUT A MONTH AND A HALF.

HE WAS KIND OF EMBARRASSED BE-
CAUSE SHE WAS BLACK, HOWEVER,
AND INTRODUCED HER TO SOME
FRIENDS AS INDIAN, WHICH DIDN'T
SIT TOO WELL WITH HER. SHE LATER
BECAME THE MODEL FOR "MARDOU
FOX" IN "THE SUBTERRANEANS,"
WHICH JACK WROTE IN 3 DAYS BUT
TOOK 5 YEARS TO PUBLISH.

ONE DAY KEROUAC WAS WITH ALENE IN A NEW
YORK RESTAURANT. GORE VIDAL WAS SITTING AT
ONE OF THE TABLES AND JACK DITCHED ALENE
FOR GORE. LATER KEROUAC CALLED VIDAL A
"POMPOUS LITTLE FAG."

I SAID, "LET'S
GET A ROOM
AROUND HERE".

THEY WENT TO THE CHELSEA HOTEL AND HAD SEX. JACK WAS SO THRILLED HE
BRAGGED ABOUT THE INCIDENT. LATER, HOWEVER, HE WAS LESS BOASTFUL.

BACK AT VIKING KEROUAC FOUND HIMSELF A FRIEND WHEN THE EDITOR ARABEL PORTER PLACED
A PORTION OF "ON THE ROAD" IN THE PAPERBACK ANTHOLOGY "NEW WORLD WRITING."

THANKS, THIS'LL
DO ME A LOT
OF GOOD.

ACTUALLY, IT DIDN'T DO HIM A BIT OF GOOD, AS HE USED A PSEUDONYM WHEN IT WAS PUBLISHED.

WHO IS THIS JEAN-LOUIS ?

NEVER HEARD OF HIM.

FEBRUARY 1954 FOUND JACK AT THE CASSADYS' SOUTHERN CALIFORNIA HOME, WHERE JACK GAVE NEAL AND CAROLYN A LECTURE ON HIS RECENT INTEREST, BUDDHISM.

SEE, DHARMA MEANS...

NOT TO BE UNDONE, NEAL HIPPED JACK TO POPULAR CLAIRVOYANT EDGAR CAYCE.

HE'S LEGIT. HIS STUFF IS ADVERTISED IN A MILLION MAGAZINES.

NEAL HAD ANOTHER HERO, THE EVANGELIST ORAL ROBERTS, WHO JACK DESPISED.

OKIE HORSESHIT !!

THE PIONEERING INFLUENCE THAT JACK, GINSBERG, AND GARY SNYDER HAD IN SPREADING BUDDHISM IS NOT TO BE TAKEN LIGHTLY.

IN 1954 KEROUAC MOVED FROM CASSADY'S HOME TO SAN FRANCISCO, WHERE HE HOLED UP IN A CHEAP HOTEL ROOM AND WROTE HIS FIRST POETRY VOLUME, "SAN FRANCISCO BLUES."

THEN BACK TO NEW YORK IN APRIL. THIS TIME KEROUAC WASN'T FLAT BROKE; HE WAS RECEIVING UNEMPLOYMENT COMPENSATION FOR RAILROAD JOBS HELD IN CALIFORNIA. HE THEN STARTED A NEW CAMPAIGN TO GET HIS PROSE AND POETRY PUBLISHED. HE GOT A NEW AGENT, STERLING LORD, WHO WORKED WITH HIM UNTIL JACK'S DEATH.

LORD'S AN AWFUL QUIET GUY FOR AN AGENT, BUT LET'S SEE WHAT HE CAN DO FOR ME. THEY SAY STILL WATER RUNS DEEP.

KEROUAC FELT GREAT ABOUT THE QUALITY OF HIS WORK, BUT TRY AS LORD MIGHT HE COULDN'T SELL IT. IF THAT WEREN'T BAD ENOUGH, JOAN HAVERTY PUT OUT A WARRANT FOR HIS ARREST FOR LACK OF SUPPORT.

SUFFERING DEEPLY DUE TO HIS ALCOHOL AND DRUG EXCESSES, KEROUAC HAD PHLEBITIS. AT THE TRIAL THE JUDGE THOUGHT KEROUAC WAS IN SUCH BAD SHAPE THAT HE SET ASIDE THE CASE.

THE FIRST PART OF 1955 FOUND KEROUAC IN NORTH CAROLINA. JACK'S SISTER AND BROTHER-IN-LAW OPENED A TV STORE THERE AND MADE JACK WORK TO EARN HIS KEEP.

CLEARANCE

FINALLY JACK STARTED TO RECEIVE GOOD NEWS. SOME OF HIS PIECES WERE GETTING IN A COUPLE OF MAGAZINES, INCLUDING GEORGE PLIMPTON'S "PARIS REVIEW."

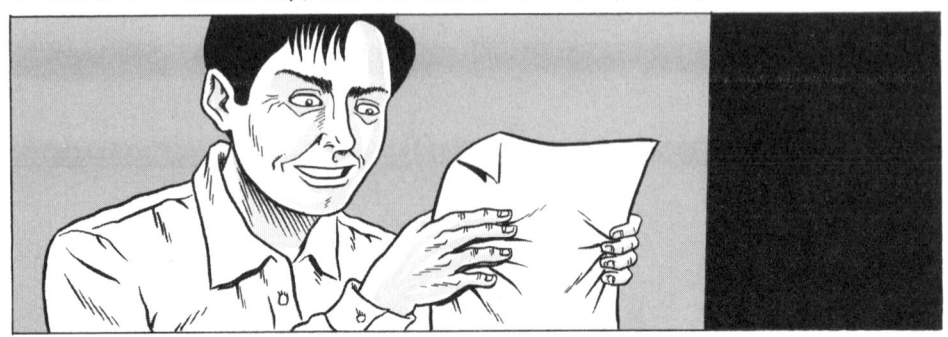

IN THE SUMMER OF 1955 KEROUAC TOOK OFF FOR MEXICO, WHERE HE GOT INVOLVED WITH A 28-YEAR-OLD PROSTITUTE. HE WROTE BEAUTIFULLY ABOUT THIS EXPERIENCE IN "TRISTESSA."

ALSO IN MEXICO, KEROUAC WROTE "MEXICO CITY BLUES," HIS FINEST POETIC VOLUME. DESPITE GINSBERG'S ASSISTANCE, HE COULDN'T SELL IT.

JACK, "MEXICO CITY BLUES" IS GREAT; IT'S A BREAKTHROUGH FOR YOU.

NOW THE SCENE SHIFTS TO GINSBERG. ALLEN GINSBERG WENT TO COLUMBIA AND OFTEN SAW KEROUAC AROUND THERE, THOUGH GINSBERG WAS FOUR YEARS YOUNGER. HE WAS A HOMOSEXUAL BUT DIDN'T KNOW WHAT TO DO ABOUT IT.

GINSBERG, A BRILLIANT STUDENT, DECIDED HE'D LIKE TO BE A POET, FOLLOWING IN THE FOOTSTEPS OF HIS FATHER, LOUIS GINSBERG, A SEMI-ACCOMPLISHED POET.

HE WORKED VERY HARD TO LEARN THE TECHNIQUES OF CLASSICAL AND ROMANTIC POETS, AND TURNED OUT VERY GOOD, THOUGH DERIVATIVE WORK.

I WON SOME POETRY PRIZES AT COLUMBIA, BUT MY FIRST APPEARANCE IN A NATIONALLY DISTRIBUTED PUBLICATION WAS "PULL MY DAISY" WHICH I DID WITH KEROUAC IN "NEUROTICA"... (1950)

THIS POEM CAME OUT LIKE I WANTED IT TO, BUT THERE SEEMS TO BE SOMETHING MISSING HERE.

FINALLY HE DECIDED TO SEARCH FOR MORE ORIGINALITY. HE BECAME STRONGLY INFLUENCED BY WALT WHITMAN, WILLIAM CARLOS WILLIAMS, AND T. S. ELIOT.

YEAH, THERE'S NO DOUBT THAT I HAVE TO BRING MY STYLE INTO THE TWENTIETH CENTURY.

THE WASTE LAND
TS ELIOT

HE WAS PARTICULARLY INTERESTED IN WILLIAMS BECAUSE BOTH CAME FROM THE SAME CITY—PATERSON, NEW JERSEY—AND WILLIAMS CAME TO ADMIRE ALLEN GREATLY...

DON'T GO IN FOR SHOW-OFFY STUFF, GET RIGHT INTO THE HEART OF WHAT YOU'RE TRYING TO DO— REMEMBER, NO IDEAS BUT IN THINGS.

33

AFTER GRADUATING, GINSBERG GOT LOW-PAYING JOBS WHILE HE HUNG AROUND WITH THE SAME BOHEMIAN CROWD.

HE HAD A ROUGH TIME DURING AND RIGHT AFTER COLLEGE. HE'D BEEN IN TROUBLE A COUPLE OF TIMES, ONCE FOR LETTING THIEVES, INCLUDING HUNCKE, USE HIS APARTMENT TO STASH THEIR STOLEN GOODS. FOR THIS HE WAS TRIED.

WELL, WELL, WHAT HAVE WE HERE?

HE WASN'T SENT TO PRISON BUT INSTEAD TO COLUMBIA PRESBYTERIAN PSYCHIATRIC HOSPITAL, WHERE HE MET THE PATIENT CARL SOLOMON, TO WHOM HE WOULD DEDICATE "HOWL."

I'M MYSHKIN.

I'M KIRILOV.

IN 1954 GINSBERG MOVED TO THE SAN FRANCISCO AREA, NOT SURE OF WHAT TO DO. HE DID MARKET RESEARCH FOR A TIME.

THERE HE MET HIS LONGTIME LOVER, PETER ORLOVSKY, AT THE HOME OF PAINTER ROBERT LAVIGNE.

GINSBERG THEN BEGAN WORKING ON THE POEM THAT WOULD BECOME "HOWL," AND HE SENT IT TO JACK.

THIS IS A MIGHTY GOOD WORK BUT HE NEVER SHOULD HAVE EDITED IT...

JACK HITCHHIKED AND BUSSED FROM MEXICO CITY TO THE BAY AREA IN SEPTEMBER. HIS LAST RIDE WAS FROM A BEAUTIFUL BLONDE, WHO DROVE 110 MPH AND WORE A BATHING SUIT. HE IMMORTALIZED HER IN HIS POEM "GOOD BLONDE."

IN NOVEMBER COWLEY WROTE JACK ABOUT SOME LEGAL PROBLEMS WITH "ON THE ROAD" THAT TOOK EIGHTEEN MONTHS TO RESOLVE.

OH, NO, NOT SOMETHING ELSE.

NONETHELESS, JACK HAD A GREAT TIME IN SAN FRANCISCO, BECOMING ACQUAINTED WITH A BUNCH OF FINE YOUNG POETS AND HANGING OUT WITH GINSBERG.

THIS BUILT TO THE MOMENTOUS POETRY READING ON OCTOBER 7, 1955, AT THE SIX GALLERY, WITH GINSBERG, PHILIP LAMANTIA, GARY SNYDER, MICHAEL McCLURE, AND PHILIP WHALEN. IT WAS HERE THAT GINSBERG GAVE HIS POWERFUL READING OF "HOWL".

I SAW THE BEST MINDS OF MY GENERATION DESTROYED...

JACK HAD A GREAT TIME, THOUGH HE WAS TOO SHY TO READ. HE COLLECTED MONEY FROM THE CROWD FOR CHEAP WINE, AND DISTRIBUTED IT AROUND THE GALLERY AS HE CHEERED THE POETS ON.

GO GO GO!

OVERNIGHT, GINSBERG WAS IN DEMAND. POET-PUBLISHER LAWRENCE FERLINGHETTI SENT GINSBERG A TELEGRAM READING, "I GREET YOU AT THE BEGINNING OF A NEW CAREER. WHEN DO I GET THE MANUSCRIPT?"

TELEGRAMS YET!

McCLURE SAID THE DAY AFTER THE READING THAT GINSBERG HAD TURNED FROM A NEBBISH TO AN "EPIC VOCAL BARD." HIS READING OF "HOWL" HAD TO HAVE CREATED MORE INTEREST IN POETRY AND THE BEATS THAN ANYTHING IN MEMORY.

YOU'RE SOMEBODY, MAN.

FERLINGHETTI PUBLISHED "HOWL" AS PART OF HIS POCKET POETS SERIES AND IT WAS DISTRIBUTED ACROSS THE COUNTRY. THE BOOK WAS SEIZED BY U.S. CUSTOMS IN SAN FRANCISCO. CITY LIGHTS SECURED ITS RELEASE WITH THE HELP OF THE AMERICAN CIVIL LIBERTIES UNION. SOON THEREAFTER, THE SAN FRANCISCO POLICE DEPARTMENT CHARGED FERLINGHETTI AND HIS BOOKSTORE MANAGER, SHIGEYOSHI MURAO, ON CHARGES OF OBSCENITY FOR SELLING "HOWL" AND ANOTHER PUBLICATION. BOTH MEN WERE EVENTUALLY FOUND INNOCENT ON ALL CHARGES.

WHILE THESE TRIALS WERE GOING ON, GINSBERG WAS OUT OF THE COUNTRY. WHEN HE CAME BACK TO THE U.S.A., THOUGH, HE'D BECOME ONE OF THE WORLD'S MOST FAMOUS POETS.

AS FOR JACK, HE HUNG AROUND SAN FRANCISCO AFTER OCTOBER 7 AND MADE SOME GOOD FRIENDS, LIKE SNYDER AND WHALEN.

HE LEFT BEFORE CHRISTMAS 1955 TO GET BACK TO NORTH CAROLINA SO HE COULD CELEBRATE THE HOLIDAY, TRAVELING BY HITCHHIKING AND RIDING FREIGHT TRAINS.

EARLY IN 1956 JACK COMPLETED "VISIONS OF GERARD," A MOVING STORY OF HIS OLDER BROTHER, WHO HAD DIED AT AGE NINE. THIS WAS HIS FIRST OF SEVERAL BOOKS WHERE THE PROTAGONIST, A THINLY DISGUISED KEROUAC, WAS NAMED DULUOZ.

ON FEBRUARY 7, 1956, KEROUAC WAS OFFERED A JOB LATER IN THE YEAR AS A FIRE LOOKOUT IN WASHINGTON STATE. HE GRABBED THE OPPORTUNITY AND WORKED FROM JUNE TO AUGUST AT A PLACE CALLED DESOLATION RIDGE.

IN APRIL 1956, KEROUAC TRAVELED BACK TO CALIFORNIA TO STAY IN SNYDER'S CABIN. SNYDER WAS ABOUT TO LEAVE FOR TWELVE YEARS OF TRAINING IN ZEN BUDDHISM. KEROUAC REALLY RESPECTED THE YOUNGER MAN.

KEROUAC WAS IN NEW YORK ON SEPTEMBER 5, 1957, IN TIME TO READ GILBERT MILSTEIN'S RAVE REVIEW ABOUT THE FINALLY PUBLISHED "ON THE ROAD" IN "THE NEW YORK TIMES BOOK REVIEW." HE WAS WITH HIS GIRLFRIEND, JOYCE JOHNSON.

THE BOOK WOUND UP GETTING MIXED REVIEWS, BUT IT WAS A BESTSELLER. AMONG THE BOOK'S ADMIRERS WERE JACQUELINE KENNEDY, TOM HAYDEN, AND KEN KESEY.

IT IS GOOD, ISN'T IT?

VERY GOOD.

WE ALL TRIED TO IMITATE IT.

JACK BECAME A CELEBRITY FOR A WHILE, GOING ON TV AND MAKING JAZZ AND POETRY RECORDS.

HE WAS HAMPERED IN TRYING TO CAPITALIZE ON HIS NEW FAME, HOWEVER, BY BOOZE AND DRUGS.

REFUSE REQUESTS FOR INTERVIEWS WHEN YOU DON'T FEEL WELL.

VIKING HAD THE OPTION OF PUBLISHING KEROUAC'S NEXT NOVEL, BUT TURNED DOWN EVERYTHING HE SHOWED THEM.

"DOCTOR SAX," "MAGGIE CASSIDY," "VISIONS OF GERARD," "VISIONS OF CODY," "TRISTESSA," "THE SUBTERRANEANS," "MEXICO CITY BLUES," "SOME OF THE DHARMA," AND "OLD ANGEL MIDNIGHT"— THEY TURNED 'EM ALL DOWN.

THEY WERE ALL MORE MODERN BOOKS THAN "ON THE ROAD," WHICH IS RELATIVELY CONVENTIONAL. SINCE THEN, KEROUAC HAD BEEN USING HIS "SPONTANEOUS PROSE"STYLE, WHICH HAS STREAM-OF-CONSCIOUSNESS, TRANCE WRITING, AUTOMATIC WRITING, AND PROSE-POETRY ELEMENTS IN IT. SOME OF THE MATERIAL WAS WHAT HE HAD BEEN HOLDING BACK FOR YEARS. VIKING WANTED SOMETHING A LOT MORE TRADITIONAL, BUT JACK REFUSED TO EVOLVE BACKWARD.

"ON THE ROAD" IS OLD STUFF TO ME BY NOW.

IN 1958 NEAL CASSADY WAS ARRESTED FOR NARCOTICS POSSESSION (A COUPLE OF JOINTS) AND THROWN INTO SAN QUENTIN. JACK DIDN'T WANT TO HELP HIM MUCH, POSSIBLY FEARING BAD PUBLICITY.

I GAVE 'IM A TYPEWRITER. WHAT DO THEY WANT?

"THE SUBTERRANEANS," AN INTERESTING AND ORIGINAL BOOK ABOUT JACK'S AFFAIR WITH ALENE LEE, WAS PUBLISHED BY GROVE PRESS AND GOT PANNED. REVIEWERS REFUSED TO SEE THAT JACK'S STYLISTIC NONCONFORMITY WAS A MUCH-NEEDED INFLUENCE. THOUGH HIS GRAMMAR AND SYNTAX WERE UNCONVENTIONAL, HE DID KNOW HOW TO WRITE IN AN ORTHODOX FASHION.

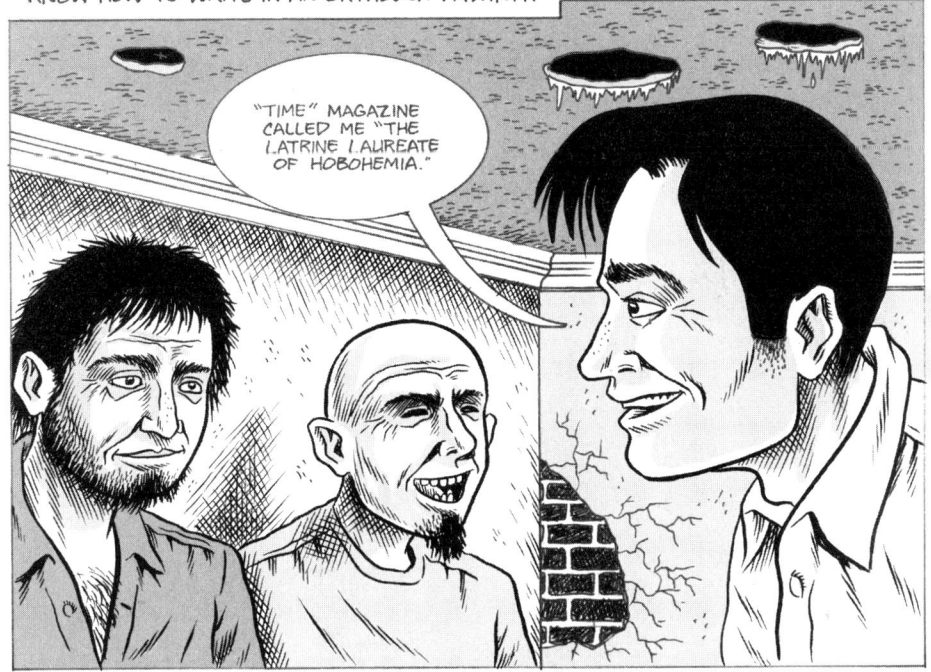

"TIME" MAGAZINE CALLED ME "THE LATRINE LAUREATE OF HOBOHEMIA."

NOW THAT JACK HAD SOME MONEY, HE BOUGHT A HOUSE FOR HIMSELF AND HIS MOTHER ON LONG ISLAND.

HOW DO YOU LIKE IT, MOM?

HE DUG THE SUBURBAN SCENE AT FIRST. A "NEWSDAY" REPORTER WROTE: "FOR THE FIRST TIME SINCE HIS BOYHOOD IN LOWELL [HE] WAS DUG IN, ROOTED OFF THE ROAD."

YEAH, I DIG MY NEIGHBORS AND THE KIDS IN THE NEIGHBORHOOD.

AS HIS LIFE SEEMED TO SETTLE DOWN, KEROUAC INCREASINGLY INSISTED THAT HE HAD ALWAYS BEEN A POLITICAL RIGHT-WINGER.

I REALLY LIKE EISENHOWER...

"A SAINT."

WHEN KEROUAC CONSULTED WITH ZEN MASTER D.T. SUZUKI IN 1958 ABOUT HIS PROBLEMS, SUZUKI SAW HE WAS AN ALCOHOLIC AND ADVISED JACK TO SWITCH TO—

GREEN TEA.

"THE DHARMA BUMS," A THOUGHTFUL AND EASY-TO-READ BOOK RELEASED IN 1958, WAS ALSO SAVAGED BY CRITICS.

A BIG SUPPORTER, THOUGH, WAS NORMAN MAILER, WHO LIKED KEROUAC'S MACHO STYLE.

KEROUAC AND GINSBERG BEGAN WORKING ON THE MOVIE "PULL MY DAISY" WITH ROBERT FRANK AND ALFRED LESLIE. KEROUAC'S NARRATION WAS OUTSTANDING. IT WAS A MILESTONE IN THE HISTORY OF INDEPENDENT FILM.

"ON THE ROAD" WAS ALSO BEING MINED FOR "BEATNIK" MATERIAL IN PROFITABLE TV SHOWS LIKE "DOBIE GILLIS" AND "ROUTE 66." KEROUAC CHARGED PLAGIARISM AND UNSUCCESSFULLY TRIED TO SUE.

JACK CONTINUED LIVING WITH HIS MOTHER, BUT BOUGHT HER A SERIES OF HOUSES FROM NEW YORK STATE TO FLORIDA. IT MADE HIM FEEL LIKE HE WAS PAYING HER BACK.

THIS PIE IS TERRIFIC, MOM; WHAT A GEM YOU ARE.

MAKING PERIODIC TRIPS FROM HIS HOME, HE WAS IN DEMAND AND WENT TO ALL SORTS OF PARTIES AND SOIREES AT WHICH HE WAS FREQUENTLY DRUNK. OF COURSE HE WAS DRUNK IN PLENTY OF OTHER PLACES, TOO.

44

1960 WAS A ROUGH YEAR FOR JACK. HE WAS FREQUENTLY SICK AND SUFFERED FROM WRITER'S BLOCK.

I'VE RUN OUT OF THINGS TO SAY.

KEROUAC DID GET A KICK, AFTER KENNEDY WAS ELECTED, TO HEAR FIRST LADY JACKIE REMARK:

I READ EVERYTHING FROM COLETTE TO KEROUAC.

FIVE OF KEROUAC'S WORKS WERE RELEASED IN 1960 BY VARIOUS PUBLISHERS, BUT THEY WENT LARGELY UNNOTICED BY THE PRESS AND PUBLIC.

MAYBE I'M COMPETING WITH MYSELF, PUTTING OUT TOO MANY BOOKS AT ONCE.

KEROUAC WAS ENRAGED BY HIS EXCLUSION FROM THE HOT AUTHORS' CLUB.

CRITICS ARE A BUNCH OF MARXISTS AND FAGS.

HOWEVER, HE RECOVERED IN 1961, WRITING "BIG SUR," CALLED "ONE OF THE MOST HONEST AND SHOCKING NOVELS OF HIS CAREER." MANY CRITICS, HOWEVER, CRITICIZED THE BOOK BECAUSE HE ADMITTED HE WAS A DRUNK.

IT'S A STUPID, SHITTY BOOK.

THAT YEAR HE TOOK A TRIP BACK TO LOWELL FOR A TEN-DAY VACATION. IT STARTED OFF BADLY WHEN HIS FRIENDS CHEWED HIM OUT.

WHAT THE FUCK, YOU DOPE, YOU'RE IN LOWELL.

DURING HIS STAY HE PROPOSED TO STELLA SAMPAS, SAMMY'S SISTER, WHO HAD REMAINED IN LOWELL WHILE WORKING IN LOCAL FACTORIES. THEY DID GET MARRIED, BUT NOT TILL 1966, WHEN JACK'S MOTHER WAS INCAPACITATED.

IN 1963, "VISIONS OF GERARD," HIS TOUCHING ALTHOUGH SOMEWHAT SENTIMENTAL, PORTRAIT OF HIS BROTHER WAS FINALLY PUBLISHED. MUCH OF IT HAD BEEN WRITTEN DECADES EARLIER.

AH, GERARD, HE DIED SO YOUNG.

AS TIME WENT ON, KEROUAC HAD LESS AND LESS IN COMMON WITH THE OTHER BEATS. HE WAS SICK OF GREENWICH VILLAGE AND THE PEOPLE WHO HE CALLED "COMMUNIST JEWS." KEROUAC HAD BEEN SOMEWHAT OF A BIGOT ALL HIS LIFE, BUT NOW HE EXPRESSED HIS FEELINGS MORE AND MORE OPENLY.

HIS DREAM WAS TO SETTLE COMFORTABLY IN LOWELL AND LEAD A QUIET LIFE FOR THE REST OF HIS DAYS.

AH, THIS IS THE TICKET.

47

DURING THE 1960'S, KEROUAC HAD AN IN-FLUENCE ON THE LYRIC WRITING OF MANY POP AND ROCK SINGERS. BUT HE COULD NOT SEEM TO RECOGNIZE THOSE MUSICAL REBELS WHO ADMIRED AND READ HIM. WHEN HE HEARD OF DYLAN'S INTEREST IN HIM HE SAID:

ANOTHER FUCKING FOLK SINGER.

IN 1964 INTEREST IN KEROUAC'S WORK HAD DIMINISHED CONSIDERABLY. THERE WAS LITTLE DEMAND FOR HIS BOOKS.

AROUND THAT TIME KEROUAC WAS GOING WITH ANOTHER PUBLISHER, COWARD-MCCANN. HE OFFERED THEM "DESOLATION ANGELS," WRITTEN IN 1956-61, AND A MUCH SHORTER NOVEL, "AN AMERICAN PASSED HERE." KEROUAC'S EDITOR, ELLIS AMBURN, WANTED TO COMBINE THEM.

CAN'T YOU GET ME MORE MONEY FOR THE TWO BOOKS PUBLISHED SEPARATELY ???

NO, THAT'S ALL I CAN GET YOU.

ONCE JACK COMPRESSED THEM INTO ONE VOLUME, AMBURN WAS VERY EXCITED, BE-LIEVING IT TO BE A MASTERPIECE. AND IT IS, ONE OF KEROUAC'S MOST FULLY REALIZED PROJECTS.

BUT IT GOT THE USUAL LOUSY REVIEWS. CRITICS WERE SO NASTY TO KEROUAC, WHAT HAD HE DONE TO THEM? "DESOLATION ANGELS" WAS A COMPLEX BOOK BUT AN EASY READ. WHAT DID PEOPLE WANT?

MEANWHILE, JACK WAS MOVING ALL OVER THE PLACE AND, IN 1967, WENT BACK TO LIVE IN LOWELL WITH HIS BRIDE, STELLA.

STELLA PROVED TO BE A WONDERFUL WIFE. SHE TOOK CARE OF JACK AND HIS MOTHER, AND EVERYONE DESCRIBED HER AS TACTFUL, INTELLIGENT, AND WARM.

IN 1968 JACK WROTE AND HAD PUBLISHED "THE VANITY OF DULUOZ," WHICH COVERED HIS LIFE FROM 1935 TO 1946. JACKIE KENNEDY WENT JOB HUNTING AND ASKED AMBURN:

IN EARLY 1968 CASSADY, WHO HAD BEEN DRIVING A BUS FOR THE NOVELIST KEN KESEY, DIED SUDDENLY. AT FIRST KEROUAC SAID:

> I DON'T BELIEVE IT. WHEN NEAL WANTS TO SKIP OUT ON A WIFE OR SOMETHING HE JUST DISAPPEARS.

A FEW DAYS LATER, AMBURN WROTE, WHEN THE NEWS OF CASSADY'S DEATH WAS VERIFIED, KEROUAC CALLED HIM IN TEARS, SAYING, "I LOVED NEAL MORE THAN ANYONE IN THE WORLD. HE INSPIRED EVERY WORD I WROTE."

ON OCTOBER 20, 1969, KEROUAC WAS ADMITTED TO THE HOSPITAL. HE WAS IN SUCH BAD SHAPE, THE DOCTORS COULDN'T SAVE HIM. ON THE DEATH CERTIFICATE, THE CAUSE OF DEATH WAS GASTROINTESTINAL HEMORRHAGE DUE TO BLEEDING GASTRIC VIEARIS FROM CIRRHOSIS OF THE LIVER DUE TO EXCESSIVE ALCOHOL INTAKE FOR MANY YEARS.

ALLEN GINSBERG

WHEN WE LAST DEALT WITH GINSBERG, HE HAD JUST SCORED A HUGE SUCCESS WITH HIS *OCTOBER 7, 1955*, READING OF "HOWL" IN SAN FRANCISCO. LET'S GO BACK TO JUNE, 1926, THOUGH, WHEN HE WAS BORN. RAISED IN PATERSON, NEW JERSEY, HE WAS IN HIGH SCHOOL WHAT WE CALL A NERD, A BRILLIANT STUDENT BUT SHY, A SOCIAL FUCKUP.

HIS FATHER, LOUIS, A SOCIALIST, TAUGHT HIGH SCHOOL. HIS MOTHER, NAOMI, HAD BEEN A COMMUNIST AND ALWAYS ARGUED WITH HER HUSBAND ABOUT POLITICS. SHE WAS ALSO PSYCHOLOGICALLY ILL, AND WAS TO BECOME MORE TROUBLED AS THE YEARS WENT BY. ONE OF THE THINGS THAT ALWAYS BOTHERED GINSBERG WAS THAT HIS FATHER LET THE DOCTORS PERSUADE HIM TO SIGN FOR HER LOBOTOMY.

SOME OF GINSBERG'S LIFE BEFORE "HOWL" WAS INEXTRICABLY TIED UP WITH KEROUAC'S AND HAS BEEN DISCUSSED PREVIOUSLY. AFTER "HOWL", HOWEVER HE SLOWLY BE- CAME ONE OF THE BEST POETS IN THE WORLD AND A BONA FIDE CELEBRITY.

THANKS VERY MUCH FOR COMING, LADIES AND GENTLEMEN.

BEFORE AND DIRECTLY AFTER GRADUATING FROM COLUMBIA IN 1948, HE HELD VARIOUS JOBS, AS A WELDER, A FLUNKY ON A FREIGHTER, A WORKER FOR THE ASSOCIATED PRESS, A REPORTER FOR THE "LABOR HERALD" (AN AMERICAN FEDERATION OF LABOR PUBLICATION), AND AS A LABORER IN A RIBBON FACTORY.

IN LATE 1953 GINSBERG WENT ON THE ROAD TO FLORIDA; CUBA; SOUTHERN MEXICO, WHERE HE VISITED THE MAYAN RUINS; SOUTHERN CALIFORNIA, WHERE HE VISITED NEAL AND CAROLYN CASSADY; AND THEN TO SAN FRANCISCO, WHERE HE STAYED FOR SOME TIME.

GINSBERG GOT A JOB IN MARKET RESEARCH THERE AND STARTED AN AFFAIR WITH A 22-YEAR-OLD WOMAN, WHICH WAS GREAT UNTIL HE TOLD HER HE'D HAD SEX WITH MEN.

YOU DID **WHAT!**

MEANWHILE, HE STUCK WITH HIS POETRY, EMPLOYING OPEN FORM WITH SYLLABLE- AND VARIABLE BREATH-STOP LENGTH. HE WAS SHOWING THE INFLUENCE OF WILLIAM CARLOS WILLIAMS, AND HIS STYLE BECAME FAR MORE MODERN.

I'M TIRED OF WRITING THAT ACADEMIC-SOUNDING STUFF.

SOON, HE AND PETER ORLOVSKY BECAME A COUPLE, BUT THEIR RELATIONSHIP WAS OFTEN TROUBLED, PARTLY BECAUSE ORLOVSKY WAS BASICALLY HETEROSEXUAL AS WELL AS UNSTABLE.

YOU EXPECT ME TO DO ALL THE WORK AROUND HERE.

WELL, I'M NOT, I'M TELLING YOU I'M NOT.

NOW, NOW... CALM DOWN, PETER.

SINCE GETTING INVOLVED IN THE BOHEMIAN SCENE IN 1944, GINSBERG HAD TAKEN A LOT OF NARCOTICS, AND HANDLED THEM PRETTY WELL. HE WAS REALLY INTO EXPANDED CONSCIOUSNESS AND, AS SOON AS HE BECAME NATIONALLY PROMINENT, ADVOCATED MAKING MARIJUANA LEGAL. VARIOUS GOVERNMENT AGENCIES WERE ALWAYS TRYING TO BUST HIM.

TAKING ADVANTAGE OF THE SUCCESS OF "HOWL," GINSBERG READIED A PAMPHLET CALLED "HOWL AND OTHER POEMS" FOR LAWRENCE FERLINGHETTI AT CITY LIGHTS. IT WAS PUBLISHED IN 1956 AND IMMEDIATELY BECAME CITY LIGHTS' BEST SELLER— AND REMARKABLY, FOR POETRY, REMAINED A HUGE SELLER FOR YEARS.

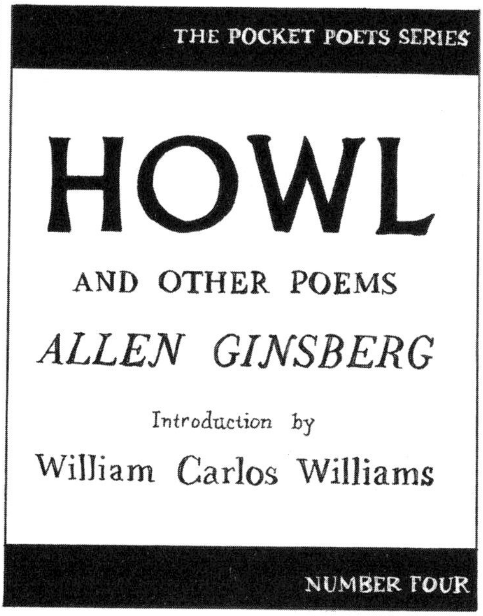

THE POCKET POETS SERIES

HOWL

AND OTHER POEMS

ALLEN GINSBERG

Introduction by

William Carlos Williams

NUMBER FOUR

HOWEVER, IT WASN'T ALL PEACHES AND CREAM FOR GINSBERG. ON JUNE 9, 1956, HE LEARNED OF HIS MOTHER'S DEATH IN A MENTAL HOSPITAL. SHE HAD BEEN ILL FOR MANY YEARS AND SHE AND LOUIS GINSBERG HAD BEEN DIVORCED. HER DEATH SHOCKED ALLEN, WHO LATER WROTE ONE OF HIS GREATEST POEMS, "KADDISH," FOR HER.

MONEY WOULD BE A PROBLEM FOR ALLEN THROUGH MUCH OF HIS LIFE, AND DESPITE "HOWL"'S SUCCESS, HE SIGNED ON FOR ANOTHER PERIOD WORKING ON A SHIP HEADED FOR THE ARCTIC. GINSBERG READ FOR THE FIRST TIME THE TORAH (KNOWN TO CHRISTIANS AS THE OLD TESTAMENT), HOPING TO MAKE SENSE OF HIS LIFE AFTER HIS MOTHER'S DEATH.

IN JANUARY 1957, GINSBERG AND ORLOVSKY LEFT FOR A LONG TOUR THAT WOULD TAKE THEM TO MEXICO, NEW YORK, AND EUROPE.

ALLEN AND PETER FIRST WENT TO L.A., WHERE ALLEN SILENCED A DRUNKEN HECKLER BY TAKING OFF HIS CLOTHES AT A READING AND CHALLENGING THE HECKLER TO TAKE OFF HIS.

WELL, GO ON AND DO SOMETHING REALLY BRAVE, TAKE OFF YOUR CLOTHES.

THEN ALLEN TRAVELED TO MEXICO CITY TO MEET KEROUAC AND THEN TO NEW YORK, WHERE HE CONNECTED WITH OLD FRIENDS AND WENT TO WORK TRYING TO GET PUBLICITY FOR HIMSELF AND THEM.

IN HIS TRAVELS HE MET SALVADOR DALI.

I'LL NEVER READ FOR MONEY.

NONSENSE. THE MEASURE OF GENIUS IS GOLD.

ON FEBRUARY 15 GINSBERG SAILED FOR TANGIER, WHERE HE MET UP AGAIN WITH KEROUAC AND BURROUGHS, WHO'D BEEN THERE FOR SOME TIME.

THERE BURROUGHS FOUND THE DOPE PLENTIFUL AND CHEAP, AS WERE THE YOUNG BOY PROSTITUTES.

HE WAS WORKING ON THE MANUSCRIPT FOR "NAKED LUNCH" BUT HAD STREWN THE PAGES ALL OVER THE ROOM. ALLEN PUT THE PAGES IN ORDER AND EDITED AND TYPED THEM. ONE OBSERVER GAVE HIM MORE CREDIT FOR "NAKED LUNCH" THAN BURROUGHS.

THEN TO SPAIN AND VENICE, WHERE THEY WENT SIGHTSEEING AND VISITED FAMOUS MUSEUMS. ALLEN WAS THRILLED TO SEE THE PAINTINGS IN PERSON. HE HAD A HUGE AMOUNT OF CURIOSITY, WHICH WAS JUST BEGINNING TO BE ASSUAGED.

BACK IN THE STATES FERLINGHETTI WAS PUT ON TRIAL FOR PUBLISHING PUR- PORTEDLY OBSCENE MATERIAL: "HOWL".

HELPED BY THE ACLU AND SUPPORTIVE SCHOLARS AND POETS, "HOWL" WAS FOUND TO BE NOT OBSCENE.

CASE CLOSED.

THE TRIAL GAVE GINSBERG WIDESPREAD PUBLICITY, AND HE BECAME THE FIRST BEAT KNOWN THROUGHOUT THE COUNTRY.

YEAH, I HEARD OF GINSBERG. WHO HASN'T?

GINSBERG TOURED ITALY AND FRANCE, THEN STARTED TO WRITE POETRY AGAIN, BEGINNING WITH "KADDISH."

"FAREWELL / WITH A LONG BLACK SHOE..."

ON TO ENGLAND, WHERE, IN FEBRUARY 1958, HE MET POETS AND ACADEMICS AND RECORDED SOME OF HIS OWN WORK.

"I SAW THE BEST MINDS OF MY GENERATION..."

AFTER A RETURN VISIT TO PARIS HE CAME BACK TO LONDON, WHERE HE MET W. H. AUDEN AND DAME EDITH SITWELL, WHO INVITED HIM TO LUNCH.

I'M EDITING AN ANTHOLOGY OF POETRY THAT WILL BE ILLUSTRATED BY PORTRAITS OF POETS IN THE NUDE.

TEE-HEE. I GRACIOUSLY DECLINE.

BACK IN FRANCE, ALLEN VISITED LOUIS FERDINAND CELINE, THE GREAT AUTHOR AND NOTORIOUS ANTI-SEMITE. ALLEN COULD TOLERATE SOME ANTI-SEMITISM, PARTICULARLY FROM WRITERS LIKE CELINE, EZRA POUND, AND KEROUAC.

I KEEP MY DOGS BECAUSE OF THE JEWS.

FINALLY, IN JULY 1958, ALLEN SAILED FOR HOME. HE RETURNED A CELEBRITY, HIS LUSTER ADDED TO BY KEROUAC, WHO HAD FINALLY HAD "ON THE ROAD" PUBLISHED. ALL THE REPORTERS WANTED TO HEAR ABOUT THE BEATS.

WHO IS THE KING OF THE BEATS, YOU OR KEROUAC.

UH

WHEN JACK'S MOTHER, WITH WHOM HE WAS LIVING, INTERCEPTED A LETTER FROM ALLEN THAT SHE THOUGHT SCANDALOUS, SHE WROTE HIM BACK, THREATENING CRIMINAL ACTION. WHEN PETER ORLOVSKY ASKED JACK TO MEET ALLEN, WHO WAS HIDDEN IN THE BUSHES NEAR JACK'S HOME, JACK WAS AFRAID TO.

UH, COULD YOU COME OUT AND VISIT ALLEN? HE'S IN THE BUSHES.

ARE YOU KIDDIN'? MY MOM WOULD FLIP OUT.

AFTER RECONCILING DIFFERENCES WITH HIS FATHER OVER THE POEM, "KADDISH AND RELATED POEMS" WAS FINALLY ISSUED IN 1961. IT GOT MIXED EARLY REVIEWS BUT WAS, WITHIN A FEW YEARS, RECOGNIZED AS A MASTERPIECE.

STRANGE NOW TO THINK OF YOU...

click! click! click!
CLICK! CLICK! CLICK! C
CLICK! CLICK! CLICK! CLIC
CLICK! CLICK! CLICK! CLICK! C
CLICK! CLICK! CLICK! CLICK! CL
CLICK! CLICK! CLICK! CLICK! CLICK
CLICK! CLICK! CLICK! CLICK! CLIC

IN 1960 GINSBERG MET DR. TIMOTHY LEARY AND TOOK LSD. HE WAS VERY IMPRESSED WITH ITS CONSCIOUSNESS-RAISING POSSIBILITIES AND WENT ON TO ENDORSE THE DRUG.

LSD SHOULD BE FOR EVERYONE, NOT THE PRIVILEGED FEW.

ALWAYS INTERESTED IN GAINING MORE KNOWLEDGE ABOUT DRUGS AND SPIRITUALITY, GINSBERG TOOK A TRIP TO TANGIER, THEN THROUGH EUROPE TO INDIA, TO BROADEN HIS STUDIES IN 1961 AND DID NOT RETURN TO NORTH AMERICA UNTIL 1963. IN 1961, HE TOOK A ROUND-THE-WORLD TRIP TO ENHANCE HIS SPIRITUALITY. HE ENDED UP IN INDIA AND STAYED THERE FOR TWO YEARS.

HE LEARNED A GREAT DEAL MORE ABOUT BUDDHISM IN INDIA AND THROUGH THE POET GARY SNYDER, WHO'D BEEN LIVING IN JAPAN. HE WAS EVEN ABLE TO OBTAIN AUDIENCES WITH THE DALAI LAMA. ALLEN REPORTED:

THE DALAI LAMA GAVE THE SAME ANSWER EVERYONE ELSE DID: DRUG STATES ARE REAL PSYCHIC STATES BUT AREN'T ULTIMATELY USEFUL TO YOU BECAUSE YOU DIDN'T GET THEM ON YOUR OWN WILL AND EFFORT.

NEVERTHELESS, GINSBERG RETURNED TO THE USA A MORE ENLIGHTENED HUMAN, IN HIS OWN MIND, THOUGH HE HAD RAPID MOOD SWINGS AND IRRITATED SOME PEOPLE WITH HIS MANTRA-SINGING.

OOOMMMMMMMMM.

ALLEN ALSO WANTED TO PROSELYTIZE ABOUT SEX.

FREE LOVE WILL SAVE THE WORLD.

AFTER A POETS' CONFERENCE IN VANCOUVER, GINSBERG WENT TO SAN FRANCISCO, WHERE HE SAW NEAL CASSADY, WHO HAD SERVED TWO YEARS ON A DRUG CHARGE AND WAS DEPRESSED. HE AND CAROLYN WERE GETTING DIVORCED.

YOU STILL GOING TO THE TRACK?

YEAH, BUT I'M LOSING THERE, TOO.

POLITICALLY ACTIVE, GINSBERG WAS ALSO AMONG 500 PEOPLE WHO PROTESTED THE VISIT TO THE USA OF MADAME NHU, WIFE OF THE SOON-TO-BE-ASSASSINATED PRESIDENT OF SOUTH VIETNAM WHO HAD BEEN KEPT IN POWER BY U.S. SUPPORT. GINSBERG HELD A PLACARD FOR FOURTEEN HOURS WHILE SINGING MANTRAS.

I'M HERE TODAY ON THE PICKET LINE TRYING TO BE TENDER TO MADAME NHU AND MAO TSE. OR RATHER, ASKING THEM TO BE TENDER.

EVIL

IN EARLY 1964 GINSBERG WAS INTRODUCED TO BOB DYLAN BY A REPORTER. THEY ADMIRED EACH OTHER AND HIT IT OFF. LATER THEY WOULD WORK ON PROJECTS TOGETHER.

ALLEN ALSO GOT INTO SEVERAL BATTLES IN-
VOLVING THE HARASSING OF CLUB OWNERS AND
THE POETS THAT READ THERE. HE WON. HE
ALSO GOT INVOLVED IN CASES, INCLUDING THAT
OF LENNY BRUCE, INVOLVING FIRST AMEND-
MENT RIGHTS. HE WAS HAVING A NOTICEABLE
EFFECT ON THE NEW YORK POLITICAL SCENE.

ALLEN WAS INVITED TO GO TO A HAVANA
WRITERS' CONFERENCE IN 1965 BY THE
CUBAN MINISTER OF CULTURE,
HAYDEE SANTAMARIA.

MAN, ALLEN, NOBODY
KNOWS ABOUT IT BUT
YOU'RE A PRESENCE,
YOU GET THINGS
DONE.

WE'D BE
DELIGHTED IF
YOU COULD
ATTEND.

DURING HIS FIRST DAY THERE HE WAS APPROACHED BY SOME YOUNG FELLOWS PUB-
LISHING A LITERARY MAGAZINE, "EL PUENTE," WHO COMPLAINED TO HIM ABOUT THE
PERSECUTION OF HOMOSEXUALS AND CRACKDOWNS BY THE SPECIAL POLICE UNIT,
LACRA SOCIAL.

I'LL DO
WHAT I
CAN.

THE NEXT DAY ALLEN STARTED ASKING CUBAN OFFICIALS ABOUT THE GOVERNMENT'S
ATTITUDE TOWARD HOMOSEXUALS AND MARIJUANA.

AND
ANOTHER
THING...

THOUGH CAUTIONED TO SHUT UP, GINSBERG CONTINUED TO ASK EMBARRASSING QUESTIONS, WHICH LED TO HIS BEING KICKED OUT OF THE COUNTRY.

FROM THERE ALLEN WENT TO COMMUNIST CZECHOSLOVAKIA, WHERE HE WAS A GUEST OF THE STATE, GIVEN A FREE HOTEL ROOM AND SOME SPENDING CASH. ON TOP OF THIS, GINSBERG GOT ROYALTIES ON HIS BOOKS FROM THE CZECHS.

NOT ONLY DID GINSBERG HAVE ENOUGH CASH TO HAVE A PLEASANT TIME IN CZECHOSLOVAKIA, THERE WAS MONEY LEFT TO VISIT THE USSR, WHICH HE DID.

RUSSIA WAS THE BIRTHPLACE OF GINSBERG'S MOTHER AND HIS FATHER'S GRANDPARENTS. ALSO IT WAS HOME TO SOME OF THE GREATEST LITERARY FIGURES OF ALL TIME. NATURALLY GINSBERG, A PASSIONATE TRAVELER, WOULD WANT TO SEE IT.

FIRST HE MET JOE LEVY, HIS MOTHER'S COUSIN, WHO EXPLAINED WHY, AFTER COMING TO THE USA, HE HAD GONE BACK TO RUSSIA.

MY BROTHER ISSER HAD A BALD SPOT THAT U.S. IMMIGRATION OFFICIALS INTERPRETED AS A POSSIBLE MANIFESTATION OF DISEASE.

SO A BRANCH OF THE FAMILY GOT SENT BACK TO THE SOVIET UNION.

GINSBERG ALSO MET SOME RUSSIAN POETS, INCLUDING YEVGENY YEVTUSHENKO.

HERE WE HEAR MANY SAD THINGS ABOUT YOU, THAT YOU ARE A PEDERAST, BUT I KNOW IT IS NOT TRUE.

IT'S ALL TRUE.

HE ALSO MET ANDREI VOZNESENSKY, A POET WITH A PHILOSOPHY CLOSER TO ALLEN'S. THEY WOULD MEET AGAIN IN THE USA, MEXICO CITY, AND AMSTERDAM. THEY PARTED SADLY.

I AM UNHAPPY THAT I CAN'T STAY A FEW MORE DAYS.

I AM GLAD TO SEE YOU.

WE ARE BOTH POETS ABOVE ALL ELSE. WE ARE TOGETHER. THAT'S SUPREME.

64

BACK IN CZECHOSLOVAKIA HE WAS ELECTED KING OF THE 1965 MAY DAY FESTIVAL, WHICH STARTLED OFFICIALS AND WAS PARTLY RESPONSIBLE FOR HIS BEING KICKED OUT OF THE COUNTRY. HE LATER WROTE OF THIS PERIOD IN THE POEM "KRAL MAJALES."

YOU'RE TAKING MY CROWN AWAY?

GINSBERG'S NEXT STOP WAS LONDON, WHERE HE MET WITH BOB DYLAN AND THE BEATLES. JOHN LENNON ASKED ALLEN IF HE COULD SIT CLOSER TO HIM, AND ALLEN FELL IN HIS LAP.

WHEN ALLEN GOT BACK TO AMERICA HE HIT THE GROUND RUNNING. HE ATTENDED A BERKELEY POETRY CONFERENCE, LEARNED HE WAS GOING TO BE IN AN ENGLISH POETRY FILM, AND HIS IMPRESSIVE POEM "ANGKOR WAT" WAS BEING READIED FOR PUBLICATION. HE WAS AN INTERNATIONAL CELEBRITY. THAT MAY BE WHY U.S. OFFICIALS CHECKED HIM FOR DRUGS AS SOON AS HIS PLANE LANDED.

ALLEN ALSO RECEIVED A GUGGENHEIM FELLOWSHIP, WHICH WAS WELCOME SINCE HIS CELEBRITY WASN'T MAKING HIM RICH YET, AND A LOT OF WHAT HE DID MAKE, HE GAVE AWAY TO FRIENDS AND NEEDY ORGANIZATIONS.

HERE, MAN, PAY IT BACK WHEN YOU CAN.

IN SAN FRANCISCO ALLEN MET WITH KEN KESEY AND HIS FOLLOWERS. KESEY'S BUS "FURTHUR" WAS DRIVEN BY NEAL CASSADY, SO THEY HAD A REUNION. THE SCENE WAS TOO CHAOTIC THOUGH.

GINSBERG WAS APPRISED OF CASSADY'S DEATH IN FEBRUARY 1968. NATURALLY THIS SADDENED HIM AND HE WROTE THE LOVELY POEM "ELEGY FOR NEAL CASSADY."

IN BERKELEY, GINSBERG WAS RESPONSIBLE FOR BRINGING TEMPORARY PEACE BETWEEN ANTIWAR PROTESTERS AND THE HELLS ANGELS.

IN JANUARY 1966, GINSBERG, ORLOVSKY, AND OTHERS SET OFF ON A TOUR OF THE HEART-LAND OF AMERICA, WHERE HE WROTE HIS CELEBRATED "WICHITA VORTEX SUTRA," AN ATTACK ON WAR AND RIGHT-WING POLITICS IN GENERAL. GINSBERG USED THE AUTO-POESY (IMPROVISED) STYLE TO COMPOSE IT.

THE HIPPIE REVOLUTION WAS JUST THEN BEGINNING. IN 1967 ALLEN WENT TO A ROUNDTABLE DISCUSSION IN SAN FRANCISCO WITH LEARY, GARY SNYDER, AND ALAN WATTS. THE HIPPIES WERE INTO FREE DRUGS AND SEX WITH A PASSION, AND ALLEN HAD A GREAT DEAL IN COMMON WITH THEM AND SAW THE HIPPIES' COMMUNITY GROWING FROM THE BEAT MOVEMENT.

THIS IS WHAT A BOHEMIAN REVOLUTION SHOULD BE ABOUT.

ON JUNE 14, GINSBERG TESTIFIED ABOUT DRUGS BEFORE A CONGRESSIONAL COMMITTEE. HE WAS WELL INFORMED, BUT HIS QUESTIONERS WEREN'T BUYING WHAT HE WAS SELLING, ESPECIALLY NEW YORK'S REPUBLICAN JEWISH SENATOR, JACOB JAVITS.

DO YOU CONSIDER YOURSELF QUALIFIED TO GIVE A MEDICAL OPINION WHICH WILL DETERMINE THE FATE OF MY 16-YEAR-OLD SON?

GOLDEN GATE PARK IN JANUARY 1967 HAD THE FIRST HUMAN BE-IN. MUSIC WAS SUPPLIED BY THE GRATEFUL DEAD, JEFFERSON AIRPLANE, AND QUICKSILVER MESSENGER SERVICE. 30,000 PEOPLE WERE THERE. ALL OF THIS MADE ALLEN SKEPTICAL.

WHAT IF WE'RE ALL WRONG?

YOU MEAN THAT THIS KIND OF MASS EVENT WOULD BRING THE COPS IN?

THIS WAS WHERE TIMOTHY LEARY SAID:

TURN ON TO THE SCENE, TUNE IN TO WHAT IS HAPPENING — AND DROP OUT... AND FOLLOW ME.

GINSBERG TRAVELED AND ACCOMPLISHED A LOT IN 1967. TO HELP PERSECUTED POETS, FOR EXAMPLE, HE WENT TO THE INTERNATIONAL POETRY FESTIVAL.

STRUNG OUT AND DEPRESSED, PETER ORLOVSKY CRACKED UP DURING THE SUMMER AND WAS ADMITTED FOR TREATMENT. GINSBERG RETURNED FROM EUROPE IN NOVEMBER 1967 AND TOLD HIM TO GET OFF METHEDRINE. WHEN PETER CAME HOME A WEEK LATER HE WAS OFF SPEED — FOR THE TIME BEING.

YOU LOOK GOOD.

BEGINNING IN DECEMBER, GINSBERG BEGAN ATTENDING ANTIWAR DEMONSTRATIONS.

Peace!

MAKE LOVE NOT WAR

CONCERNED ABOUT PETER'S DRUG PROBLEMS, IN 1968 GINSBERG BOUGHT A FARM OUTSIDE CHERRY VALLEY, NEW YORK, TO PUT ORLOVSKY IN A HEALTHIER ENVIRONMENT.

IT NEEDED A LOT OF WORK BUT PETER WAS A GREAT HELP IN REPAIRING THE HOUSE, PLANTING VEGETABLES, AND TAKING CARE OF A FEW GOATS, CHICKENS, AND A COW. MANY, PROBABLY TOO MANY, OF GINSBERG'S FRIENDS LOOKED UPON THE FARM AS A RETREAT AND SOMETIMES PROVED DISTRACTING.

WITH THE ASSASSINATIONS OF MARTIN LUTHER KING, JR., AND ROBERT KENNEDY AND THE POLICE RIOT AT THE DEMOCRATIC CONVENTION, 1968 PROVED A VERY EVENTFUL YEAR IN AMERICAN HISTORY. GINSBERG WAS IN CHICAGO FOR THE CONVENTION AND THE RIOT.

ON A COUPLE OF OCCASIONS WHEN THE POLICE THREATENED PEOPLE, GINSBERG BEGAN HIS BUDDHIST CHANTS AND WAS ABLE TO RESCUE THEM.

OMMMMMMMM....

AT ONE POINT GINSBERG CHANTED FOR 7 STRAIGHT HOURS TRYING TO CALM THINGS DOWN.

OMMMMMMMMMMMMMM.

GINSBERG WAS NOT ARRESTED OR BROUGHT IN FRONT OF JUDGE HOFFMAN, AS WERE THE CHICAGO 8, BUT HE GAVE ELQUENT TESTIMONY ON THEIR BEHALF. HE EVEN RECITED "HOWL."

"ANGEL-HEADED HIPSTERS BURNING FOR THE ANCIENT HEAVENLY CONNECTION..."

IN 1969, WHEN KEROUAC DIED, A BROKEN-HEARTED ALLEN ATTENDED HIS FUNERAL.

GINSBERG CONTINUED TO PROTEST THE WAR AND IN 1971 CHARGED THAT THE CIA WAS PAYING LAOS'S MEO TRIBESMEN TO FIGHT THE VIETNAMESE INSURGENTS. THE CIA DENIED THIS, BUT GINSBERG WAS LATER PROVEN CORRECT. HE ALSO POINTED OUT THAT CORRUPT SOUTH VIETNAMESE WERE PROFITING FROM A HUGE DRUG TRADE.

YOU GUYS SAID I DIDN'T KNOW WHAT I WAS TALKING ABOUT. GUESS AGAIN!!

IN LATE 1970 GINSBERG MET CHOGYAM TRUNGPA, A BUDDHIST HOLY MAN AND TEACHER, AND CHOSE HIM AS HIS GURU. CHOGYAM WAS HARDLY A TYPICAL BUDDHIST, WITH MUCH ERRATIC AND IRRESPONSIBLE BEHAVIOR. BUT HE BECAME ALLEN'S TEACHER.

70

IN RETURN GINSBERG AGREED TO BE TRUNGPA'S POETRY GURU.

IN 1972 ALLEN WENT TO THE REPUBLICAN NATIONAL CONVENTION TO PROTEST THE WAR.
HE GOT TO TALK TO HENRY KISSINGER ON THE PHONE, BUT KISSINGER WOULDN'T SET
UP A MEETING WITH PROTEST LEADERS.

TRUNGPA IN 1973 INVITED GINSBERG TO BE PART OF A SCHOOL THAT HE'D LEAD IN THE
ROCKY MOUNTAINS.

ANNE WALDMAN AND ALLEN GAVE POETRY READINGS AT TRUNGPA'S NEW NAROPA
INSTITUTE IN BOULDER, COLORADO, WITH GOOD RESULTS.

71

THEY HAD A PROBLEM WITH THE NAME, BUT WALDMAN CAME UP WITH A SOLUTION.

CALL IT THE "JACK KEROUAC SCHOOL OF DISEMBODIED POETICS."

SOUNDS GREAT.

GINSBERG TAUGHT AT THE SCHOOL IN THE SUMMERS.

TO BENEFIT THE NAROPA PROJECT, ON APRIL 17, 1975, GINSBERG GAVE A HISTORIC READING AT COLUMBIA AT WHICH HE SAID:

I WANT TO BE KNOWN AS THE MOST BRILLIANT MAN IN AMERICA.

ANOTHER HIGHLIGHT THAT YEAR WAS GINSBERG'S APPEARANCE IN BOB DYLAN'S TOURING ROLLING THUNDER REVUE. IT WAS FILMED FOR A MOTION PICTURE AS WELL.

"RENALDO AND CLARA," DYLAN'S FILM ABOUT ROLLING THUNDER, WAS RELEASED IN JANUARY 1978, TO GENERALLY UNFAVORABLE REVIEWS, BUT CRITICS LIKED GINSBERG'S APPEARANCES. SAID ONE CRITIC:

THE SCENES OF ALLEN GINSBERG READING "KADDISH" AND SINGING BLAKE POEMS... ARE THE BEST IN THE MOVIE.

THAT SPRING GINSBERG GOT AN IN-PERSON ACCOUNT OF W.S. MERWIN'S AND A FEMALE COMPANION'S VIOLENT ENCOUNTER AT NAROPA. AT ODDS WITH TRUNGPA, THEY HAD QUARRELED WHEN THE MASTER ORDERED HIS STUDENTS TO STRIP THE COUPLE NAKED, WHICH THEY DID, VERY ROUGHLY.

!

ALLEN, CAUGHT BETWEEN CRITICIZING TRUNGPA, HIS TEACHER, AND WILLFULLY OVERLOOKING THE AUTHORITARIANISM, SAID NOTHING PUBLIC ABOUT THEIR CLASH FOR A WHILE, BUT THE INCIDENT DIDN'T GO AWAY.

I SEE THAT NAROPA DIDN'T GET THE GRANT MONEY THEY HOPED FOR. I WONDER IF IT HAD TO DO WITH THAT BRAWL.

REPORTER TOM CLARK OF THE "BOULDER MONTHLY" DELVED INTO THE MATTER FURTHER, AFTER THE NOVEMBER 18, 1978, JONESTOWN MASSACRE HAD FOCUSED ATTENTION UPON IT AGAIN. HE INTERVIEWED GINSBERG FOR HIS STORY AND ALLEN, IN THE OPINION OF MANY, WENT TOO FAR TO SUPPORT TRUNGPA.

HE'S SUPPORTING BUDDHIST FASCISM!

FOR A LONG TIME THE MATTER DOGGED GINSBERG. HE BELIEVED THAT HE HAD MADE MISTAKES IN HIS INTERVIEWS, AND HE FOUND FEW SYMPATHIZERS.

CLARK NEVER LET ME SEE THE TEXT OF HIS ARTICLE TO EDIT IT BEFORE IT WAS PRINTED.

BY THE LATE 1970S, ALLEN NEVERTHELESS HAD A SMALL STAFF OF PEOPLE WORKING FOR HIM ENTHUSIASTICALLY. HE GAINED RESPECTABILITY, WINNING THE NATIONAL BOOK AWARD FOR POETRY IN 1974 AND THE 1979 NATIONAL ARTS CLUB GOLD MEDAL. OTHER AWARDS FOLLOWED.

STILL OPEN TO TRYING NEW THINGS, IN 1981 HE PERFORMED WITH THE CLASH.

LATER THAT SUMMER HE SHOCKED A RE-PORTER BY SAYING THAT HE APPROVED OF SEXUAL RELATIONS WITH STUDENTS.

I BELIEVE THE BEST TEACHING IS DONE IN BED, AND I'M INFORMED THAT'S THE CLASSICAL TRADITION.

IN JANUARY 1982 GINSBERG WORKED WITH THE CLASH AGAIN. THEY FREQUENTLY
ACCEPTED HIS RECOMMENDATIONS FOR LYRIC CHANGES. JOE STRUMMER WAS A BIG FAN.

FEEL FREE TO OFFER COMMENTS, ALLEN.

ALSO IN 1982, FAMED RECORD PRODUCER JOHN HAMMOND ISSUED A GINSBERG DOUBLE ALBUM
THAT CONTAINED PERFORMANCES CUT OVER A PERIOD OF YEARS. DYLAN APPEARED ON IT.

I AM THRILLED TO PRESENT ALLEN ON MY OWN LABEL.

ALLEN WAS STILL WRITING FINE POETRY AND CITY LIGHTS WAS STILL PUBLISHING PAMPHLETS
OF HIS WORK, OF WHICH THE ANTINUCLEAR "PLUTONIAN ODE" IS ONE OF THE MOST
WELL-KNOWN.

"WHAT NEW ELEMENT BEFORE US UNBORN IN NATURE? IS THERE A NEW THING UNDER THE SUN?"

HE CONTINUED TO TRAVEL TO HOT SPOTS, MEETING WITH, FOR EXAMPLE, DANIEL ORTEGA,
PRESIDENT OF NICARAGUA, WHILE THE U.S.-SPONSORED CONTRA WAR WAS GOING ON.

LOOK, DON'T MAKE ANY CRAZY STATEMENTS.

WE'RE ON A TIGHTROPE WITH THE U.S.

GINSBERG, YEVTUSHENKO, AND POET-PRIEST ERNESTO CARDENAL ISSUED AN APPEAL FOR FOREIGN TOLERANCE FOR NICARAGUA. IT WAS KNOWN AS "THE DECLARATION OF THREE."

IN 1984, GINSBERG WAS ON A USIA LIST OF PEOPLE WHO WERE BANNED FROM GOING ABROAD WITH GOVERNMENT SPONSORSHIP. SOME OTHERS WERE JAMES BALDWIN, DAVID BRINKLEY, WALTER CRONKITE, RALPH NADER, AND TOM WICKER.

ALSO IN 1984 GINSBERG WAS ABLE TO SEE CHINA FOR THE FIRST TIME. HE WAS AMAZED TO SEE HOW WELL THE CHINESE PEOPLE KNEW AMERICAN LITERATURE.

IN PRIVATE CONVERSATIONS HE SAID THAT HE'D LIKE TO SEE LESS INHIBITED SEXUAL RELATIONS IN CHINA.

WHAT HAPPENS IF SOMEONE ISN'T MARRIED? DO YOU WANT HIM TO BE CELIBATE?

IN 1985 GINSBERG'S "COMPLETE WORKS, 1947-1980" WERE PUBLISHED BY HARPER AND ROW.

HARPER AND ROW? IS HE SELLING OUT?

GINSBERG CONTINUED TO WRITE POETRY THROUGH THE 80'S AND 90'S UNTIL HE DIED IN 1997. ONE OF THE BEST EXAMPLES OF HIS LATER WORK IS "WHITE SHROUD," A POEM BASED ON A DREAM ABOUT HIS MOTHER, WITH MUCH REALISTIC DETAIL WRITTEN IN AN ALMOST-PROSE STYLE.

"WHAT ARE YOU DOING HERE? I ASKED, AMAZED SHE RECOGNIZED ME STILL."

GINSBERG WAS KEPT BUSY WITH HIS ACTIVISM AND CONTINUED TO FOLLOW CURRENT POLITICAL EVENTS AND ADVANCE THE CAUSES OF PEACE AND BUDDHISM. UNTIL HIS DEATH HE PUSHED FOR EQUALITY OF THE SEXES AND TO BENEFIT THE POOR AND OPPRESSED.

THAT SHOULD BE NATURAL FOR EVERYONE TODAY.

WILLIAM S. BURROUGHS

ANOTHER FAMOUS WRITER ASSOCIATED WITH THE BEATS WAS WILLIAM S. BURROUGHS. OLDER THAN MOST BEATS AND SLOWER TO MAKE WRITING HIS CAREER, BURROUGHS WAS BORN IN ST. LOUIS IN 1914.

HIS GRANDFATHER HAD INVENTED AN ADDING MACHINE AND BECAME VERY WEALTHY. WILLIAM'S FAMILY WAS NOT AS RICH, BUT THEY CERTAINLY WERE COMFORTABLE.

IN 1929 BURROUGHS ATTENDED THE LOS ALAMOS RANCH SCHOOL, WHICH HE DIDN'T FIT INTO DUE TO HIS ABHORRENCE OF OUTDOOR ACTIVITIES. THE ONLY SPORT HE ENJOYED WAS SHOOTING.

AT THE RANCH SCHOOL BURROUGHS HAD HIS FIRST TASTE OF NARCOTICS, CHLORAL HYDRATE, WHICH LITERALLY KNOCKED HIM OUT.

HE DID NOT GRADUATE FROM LOS ALAMOS, AND HAD TO ATTEND A PRIVATE SCHOOL BEFORE BEING ALLOWED TO ENTER HARVARD, WHICH HE DID IN 1932.

HE DIDN'T HAVE MUCH USE FOR HARVARD, BUT FREQUENTED THE LIBRARY, READING ENGLISH AND FRENCH CLASSICS.

AFTER GRADUATING IN 1936, HE WENT ON A TOUR OF EUROPE, WHERE HE MET AND MARRIED A 35-YEAR-OLD JEWISH WOMAN IN YUGOSLAVIA, PURPORTEDLY TO SAVE HER FROM FASCIST PERSECUTION. SHE SPENT THE WAR IN NEW YORK.

AFTER COMING BACK TO THE STATES BURROUGHS DECIDED TO RETURN TO HARVARD GRADUATE SCHOOL TO BE WITH HIS FRIEND KELLS ELVINS.

IN CAMBRIDGE HE AND ELVINS COLLABORATED ON A SATIRE ABOUT THE SINKING OF THE TITANIC CALLED "TWILIGHT'S LAST GLEAMINGS." HE HAD NO SUCCESS IN PUBLISHING THE PIECE, BUT IT LATER POPPED UP IN HIS NOVEL "NOVA EXPRESS."

"ESQUIRE" REJECTED IT. SAID IT WAS TOO SCREWY AND NOT FOR THEM.

HE DROPPED OUT OF GRAD SCHOOL AND RETURNED TO ST. LOUIS, WHERE HE BECAME A STUDENT OF THE SEMANTICIST ALFRED KORZYBSKI, WHO CLAIMED WORDS HAD LOST THEIR MEANING. BURROUGHS WOULD SPEND MUCH OF HIS CAREER TRYING TO CORRECT WHAT HE FELT WAS THE IMPROPER USE OF LANGUAGE.

MY GENERAL THEORY HAS BEEN THAT THE WORD IS LITERALLY A VIRUS AND THAT IT HAS NOT BEEN RECOGNIZED AS SUCH BECAUSE IT HAS ACHIEVED A STATE OF RELATIVELY STABLE SYMBIOSIS WITH ITS HUMAN HOST.

AFTER PEARL HARBOR BURROUGHS WAS DRAFTED, BUT HIS MOTHER KEPT HIM OUT OF THE SERVICE BY PLACING HIM IN A WASHINGTON, D.C., PSYCHIATRIC CENTER, WHERE HE WAS DECLARED "MENTALLY UNSUITABLE FOR MILITARY SERVICE."

BURROUGHS HEADED FOR CHICAGO IN 1942 AND WORKED AS AN EXTERMINATOR FOR EIGHT MONTHS. AT THAT TIME HE WAS RECEIVING A $200-A-MONTH ALLOWANCE FROM HIS FAMILY.

TWO OF BURROUGHS'S BUDDIES FROM ST. LOUIS, LUCIEN CARR AND DAVID KAMMERER, MET HIM IN CHICAGO. CARR, OF COURSE, WOULD WIND UP KILLING KAMMERER IN NEW YORK.

WHEN CARR LEFT TO ATTEND COLUMBIA UNIVERSITY, KAMMERER AND BURROUGHS FOLLOWED. HIS EXTERMINATOR JOB INTRODUCED WILLIAM TO SOME OF THE SEEDY PLACES HE HAD READ IN A BOOK THAT AFFECTED HIM STRONGLY, JACK BLACK'S "YOU CAN'T WIN." HE WAS READY TO MOVE ON.

WHEN THEY GOT TO NEW YORK, CARR INTRODUCED BURROUGHS TO FELLOW COLUMBIA STUDENT ALLEN GINSBERG, WHICH BEGAN A FIFTY-YEAR ASSOCIATION.

GINSBERG AND CARR THEN MET JACK KER-OUAC AND BEGAN TO FORM A CIRCLE THAT INCLUDED KEROUAC'S GIRLFRIEND, EDIE PARKER, AND JOAN VOLLMER.

GINSBERG AND KEROUAC CO-WROTE A NOVEL, "AND THE HIPPOS WERE BOILED IN THEIR TANKS," WHICH WAS REJECTED BY PUBLISHERS...

ANOTHER REJECTION SLIP!

AND BURROUGHS WAS STARTING ANOTHER LIFE, AS A TIMES SQUARE HUSTLER. HE FENCED STOLEN GOODS AND MORPHINE SYRETTES, AND HELD UP PEOPLE AT GUNPOINT IN THE SUBWAY.

BURROUGHS'S GUIDE TO LOW LIFE WAS HERBERT HUNCKE, WHO'D BEEN A HUSTLER FOR SOME TIME.

BURROUGHS INTRODUCED HUNCKE TO THE COLUMBIA CROWD AND THEY SOON STARTED LIVING A COMMUNAL LIFE IN AN APARTMENT NEAR THE UNIVERSITY.

JOAN VOLLMER, A JOURNALISM STUDENT, TOOK UP WITH BURROUGHS THOUGH HE WAS A HOMOSEXUAL. IT DIDN'T SEEM TO MATTER TO HER AND THEY EVENTUALLY MARRIED.

HE'S AS GOOD IN BED AS A PIMP.

VOLLMER AND BURROUGHS WERE BOTH DOING A LOT OF DOPE AND THEY EVENTUALLY GOT BUSTED. BEFORE THAT, THOUGH, THEY WORKED OUT LITTLE PLAYLETS, WHICH BURROUGHS WOULD LATER USE IN HIS BOOKS.

I'LL BE A HUNGARIAN PSYCHOANALYST, YOU BE A LESBIAN GOVERNESS.

BURROUGHS AND VOLLMER EVENTUALLY BOUGHT A 99-ACRE FARM IN NEW WAVERLY, TEXAS, AND HAD A SON. THEY INVITED HUNCKE TO JOIN THEM AND BEFORE LONG THEIR MAIN CROP WAS MARIJUANA.

OTHERS VISITING THEM INCLUDED NEAL CASSADY AND GINSBERG, WHO HAD A TERRIFIC CRUSH ON NEAL. NEAL DROVE BURROUGHS'S MARIJUANA CROP TO NEW YORK TO SELL, AND GINSBERG SHIPPED OUT WITH THE MERCHANT MARINE.

THE MARIJUANA SCHEME WAS A BUST. IT HAD TO BE WHOLESALED FOR $100 BECAUSE BURROUGHS AND VOLLMER WERE BEING WATCHED BY THE POLICE. THEY MOVED TO NEW ORLEANS, WHERE COPS RAIDED THEIR HOUSE AND FOUND STASHES OF DOPE. THEIR LAWYER GOT THEM OFF ON A TECHNICALITY BUT RECOMMENDED THEY GET OUT OF THE COUNTRY, WHICH THEY DID.

IN 1950 BURROUGHS, NOW IN MEXICO, WROTE GINSBERG THAT HE HAD ALMOST FINISHED A BOOK BASED ON HIS NEW YORK-TO-NEW ORLEANS EXPERIENCE CALLED "JUNKIE."

ON SEPTEMBER 6 BURROUGHS AND JOAN WERE BOTH DRUNK. SUPPOSEDLY JOAN WAS TAUNTING BURROUGHS ABOUT HIS MARKSMANSHIP. ANYWAY, A WATER GLASS WAS PLACED ON HER HEAD, AS IN THE WILLIAM TELL STORY, AND BURROUGHS SHOT AT IT, MISSING AND KILLING HER INSTANTLY.

BURROUGHS GOT A LAWYER TO HAVE HIM RELEASED FROM PRISON, BUT AFTER THE LAWYER GOT IN TROUBLE HIMSELF, BURROUGHS WENT TO SOUTH AMERICA FOR SIX MONTHS AND DISCOVERED THE LEGENDARY DRUG YAGE. BURROUGHS LEFT MEXICO IN AUGUST 1953 AND WENT BACK TO NEW YORK, WHERE HE MET GINSBERG, WHO'D DEVELOPED SOME CONTACTS IN THE PUBLISHING BUSINESS, INCLUDING CARL SOLOMON (AS IN "HOWL FOR CARL SOLOMON"), WHO AS AN EDITOR FOR ACE BOOKS ACCEPTED "JUNKIE."

WELL, I GOT AN $800 ADVANCE ON IT. THAT'S GOOD, ANYWAY.

"JUNKIE," BASED ON BURROUGHS'S EXPERIENCE AS AN ADDICT, DID NOT SELL PARTICULARLY WELL, BUT WAS A VERY REALISTIC AND INFORMATIVE PORTRAIT OF THE WORLD HE LIVED IN.

IT HOLDS UP VERY WELL TODAY.

"JUNKIE" WAS A FEATHER IN BURROUGHS'S CAP, SHOWING THE WORLD A FACET OF AMERICAN LIFE THAT IN THE 1950'S WAS VIRTUALLY UNKNOWN.

BURROUGHS CRAVED GINSBERG, BUT WHEN GINSBERG REJECTED HIM, HE LEFT FOR TANGIER, WHERE DOPE WAS EASILY OBTAINED, AS WERE YOUNG MALE PROSTITUTES.

HEY, MEESTER!

PREDICTABLY, BURROUGHS'S DRUG HABIT GOT WORSE. HE WAS HOOKED ON EUKADOL. FINALLY IT GOT SO BAD HE BORROWED $500 FROM HIS PARENTS IN 1956 AND SAW PIONEERING ENGLISH DOCTOR JOHN YERBURY DENT, WHO CURED HIM (FOR THE TIME BEING) WITH APOMORPHINE. IN SEPTEMBER 1956, HE RETURNED TO TANGIER.

HOME, SWEET HOME.

WHILE IN TANGIER, BURROUGHS WORKED ON "NAKED LUNCH." HE DESCRIBED TO GINSBERG HIS METHOD OF WRITING: "THIS IS ALMOST AUTOMATIC WRITING. I OFTEN SIT HIGH ON HASH FOR AS LONG AS SIX HOURS, TYPING AT TOP SPEED."

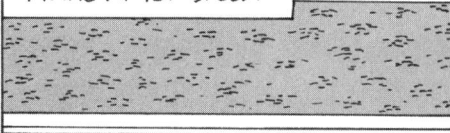

THE TITLE "NAKED LUNCH" CAME ABOUT IN AN ODD WAY. WHEN BURROUGHS WAS LIVING AROUND COLUMBIA WITH KEROUAC AND GINSBERG, HE WROTE SHORT PLAYS, OR "ROUTINES," IN WHICH THE APARTMENT DWELLERS PERFORMED. ONE DAY GINSBERG MISREAD "NAKED LUST" AS "NAKED LUNCH." KEROUAC JUMPED ON "NAKED LUNCH" AS A NOVEL TITLE. BURROUGHS SAID HE'D REMEMBER IT, AND HE DID.

JACK, ONCE MORE I AM IN YOUR DEBT.

KEROUAC VISITED BURROUGHS IN TANGIER IN FEBRUARY 1957. THE MANUSCRIPT PAGES FOR "NAKED LUNCH" WERE ALL OVER THE FLOOR, SO JACK RETRIEVED THEM AND TYPED THEM UP NEATLY. A MONTH LATER GINSBERG AND HIS NEW LOVER, PETER ORLOVSKY, CAME TO TANGIER AND EDITED "NAKED LUNCH," PUTTING THE EPISODES IN ORDER. GINSBERG WROTE TO CARR:

"IT'S QUITE A PIECE OF WRITING, ALL BILL'S ENERGY AND PROSE, PLUS OUR ORGANIZATION AND CLEANUP AND STRUCTURE."

IN JANUARY 1958, GINSBERG AND BURROUGHS WENT TO PARIS, WHERE GINSBERG SOLD "NAKED LUNCH" TO THE OLYMPIA PRESS. GROVE PRESS PUBLISHED IT IN AMERICA IN 1962, WHERE IT WAS FOUND OBSCENE SOON AFTER IT APPEARED FOR SALE. IT STAYED BANNED UNTIL A COURT DECISION IN 1966.

WELL, I HOPE ALL THIS OBSCENITY STUFF IS FINALLY OVER...

DURING THE DEBATE ABOUT THE AESTHETIC VALUE OF "NAKED LUNCH" NORMAN MAILER PROCLAIMED:

THIS TERRIBLE BORDERLAND OF SEX, SADISM, OBSCENITY, HORROR... THAT IS WHY I SALUTE MR. BURROUGHS'S WORK, BECAUSE HE HAS GONE FURTHER INTO IT THAN ANY WESTERN WRITER TODAY.

BURROUGHS HAD OTHER PROBLEMS. HIS SON WAS A DRUG ADDICT, LITERALLY GETTING HOOKED BY HIS PARENTS' PROBLEMS; BURROUGHS CAME BACK TO AMERICA TO PUT HIS SON IN THE LEXINGTON CLINIC FOR REHAB. THE STORY GOES THAT WHEN BOTH SHOWED UP AT THE ADMISSIONS DESK, THE CLERK SAID,

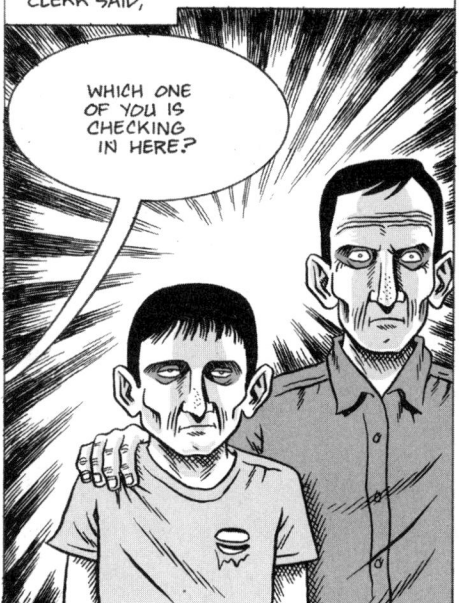

WHICH ONE OF YOU IS CHECKING IN HERE?

BILL, JR., WAS TO HAVE AN AWFUL LIFE, WHICH INCLUDED A LIVER TRANSPLANT. HE DIED IN FLORIDA IN 1981. HE SIGNED ONE LETTER TO HIS FATHER—

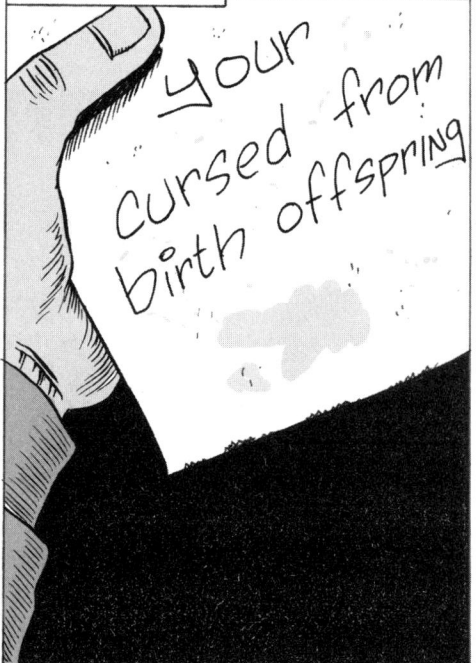

your cursed from birth offspring

A COLLABORATOR OF BURROUGHS, BRION GYSIN, ACCIDENTALLY DISCOVERED CUT-UP TECHNIQUE, A REDISCOVERY OF DADAISM. HE CUT UP SOME NEWSPAPER PAGES TO MAKE A MOUNT FOR A DRAWING AND FOUND THAT WHEN HE FIT PIECES FROM DIFFERENT PAGES TOGETHER THEY MADE SENSE, CREATING SURREAL SENTENCES. THE TECHNIQUE AIDED BURROUGHS'S ATTACK ON LINEAR STORIES AND THOUGHT PROCESSES, HE REMARKED:

CUT-UPS DESTROY OLD FALSE CONSTRUCTS AND MODELS OF REALITY.

WHILE THE DEBATE OVER "NAKED LUNCH" RAGED, BURROUGHS REALLY GOT DOWN TO WORK, PRODUCING THREE NEW NOVELS, "THE SOFT MACHINE" (1961), "THE TICKET THAT EXPLODED" (1962), AND "NOVA EXPRESS" (1964), IN WHICH HE EXPERIMENTED WITH CUT-UP AND FOLD-IN TECHNIQUES.

I'M ON A ROLL.

AS CREATIVE AS BURROUGHS WAS, HE WAS ALSO A KIND OF CRANK, A DIE-HARD MISOGYNIST AS WELL AS AN ANTI-UNION RIGHT-WINGER, SPURRED ON BY GYSIN. HE CLAIMED:

WOMEN ARE MISTAKES AND SHOULD BE ELIMINATED FROM THE POPULATION.

MEANWHILE TIMOTHY LEARY, APOSTLE OF LSD, MET WITH BURROUGHS, BUT WILLIAM HAD NO USE FOR LEARY OR THE DRUGS HE WAS CHAMPIONING. IN 1961 BURROUGHS REMEMBERED:

I HOPE NEVER TO SET EYES ON THAT HORSE'S ASS AGAIN.

IN THE SUMMER OF 1962 BURROUGHS MET WITH THE BRITISH FILMMAKER ANTONY BALCH, WHO TRIED TO USE BURROUGHS'S LITERARY TECHNIQUE IN HIS FILMS "TOWERS OPEN FIRE," "THE CUT-UPS," AND "BILL AND TONY." THOUGH THEIR QUALITY HAS BEEN QUESTIONED, THEY WERE LANDMARKS.

BILL, WOULD YOU MIND STEPPING OVER THERE?

IN THE MID-1960'S BURROUGHS OFTEN LIVED IN LONDON. IN 1967 HE DEVELOPED AN INTEREST IN SCIENTOLOGY BUT DROPPED IT.

SCIENTOLOGY WAS USEFUL TO ME UNTIL IT BECAME A RELIGION, AND I HAVE NO USE FOR RELIGION. IT'S JUST AN-OTHER ONE OF THOSE CONTROL-ADDICT TRIPS, AND WE COULD ALL DO WITHOUT THOSE.

"ESQUIRE" HIRED HIM AND OTHER CELEBRITIES TO COVER THE 1968 CHICAGO DEMOCRATIC CONVENTION, WHICH HE DIDN'T CARE A THING ABOUT.

BACK IN LONDON BURROUGHS WROTE ANOTHER NOVEL, "THE WILD BOYS", WHICH WAS EXCELLENT, THOUGH NOT AS GOOD AS HIS LAST SEVERAL BOOKS. IT FEATURES AN ATTACK ON THE FAMILY UNIT.

IT'S KIND OF A FANTASY ABOUT THE OLD WEST.

AROUND 1970, BURROUGHS STARTED GETTING ANNOYED BY BRITAIN'S CONSERVATIVE LIFESTYLE.
IN 1973 GINSBERG FOUND BURROUGHS A TEACHING JOB AT CCNY, AND HE CAME BACK TO THE USA.

GLAD YOU'RE BACK. HOPE YOU STAY A WHILE.

SOON AFTER RETURNING TO THE STATES, BURROUGHS MET JAMES GRAUERHOLZ, WHO BECAME HIS SECRETARY AND KEPT HIS AFFAIRS IN ORDER UNTIL HIS DEATH.

WHILE ON THE LECTURE CIRCUIT BURROUGHS PERFECTED AN ACT, THE DOUR, PESSIMISTIC OLD MAN.

YOU'D BE SURPRISED TO REALIZE HOW MUCH CONTROL THE GOVERNMENT HAS OVER YOUR LIFE.

INITIALLY BURROUGHS RENTED A PLACE AT 222 BOWERY, A FORMER YMCA KNOWN AS THE BUNKER. THE SINGER-POET PATTI SMITH OFTEN VISITED HIM THERE. LIKE GINSBERG, HE BECAME A HERO TO SOME ROCK STARS. HE WAS CALLED THE GODFATHER OF PUNK.

POSSIBLY BECAUSE ROCK PERFORMERS WERE OFTEN ON SOME KIND OF NARCOTIC OR ANOTHER, BURROUGHS GOT BACK ON DRUGS, BUT TOOK A METHADONE CURE.

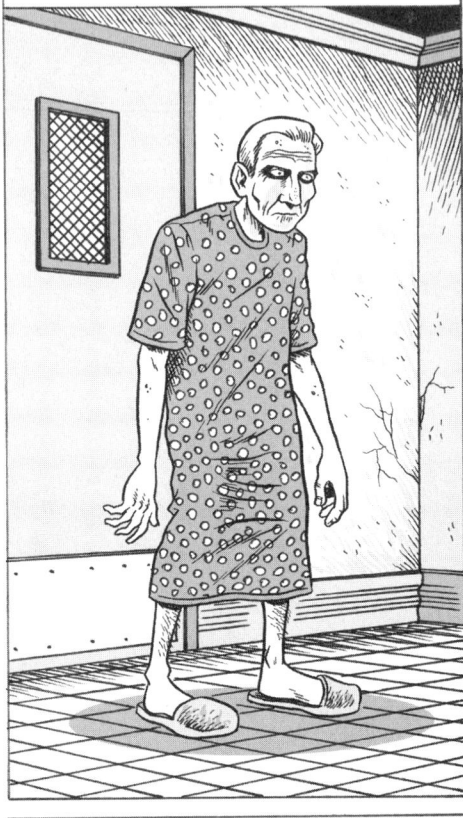

AFTER A READING IN LAWRENCE, KANSAS, GRAUERHOLZ'S HOME, HE NOTED, "THAT PLACE IN KANSAS COULD BE A NICE SPOT FOR OLD AGE," AND BOUGHT A HOUSE THERE.

IN 1981 BURROUGHS PUBLISHED "CITIES OF THE RED NIGHT," WHICH IS CONSIDERED ONE OF HIS FINEST NOVELS. IT'S UNIQUE IN BEING INFLUENCED BY BOYS' ADVENTURE STORIES, WESTERNS, MYSTERIES, PIRATE TALES, AND SCIENCE FICTION.

RADIOACTIVE VIRUS.

OTHER SUBSTANTIAL BOOKS FOLLOWED, "THE PLACE OF DEAD ROADS" (1984) AND "THE WESTERN LANDS" (1987). HERE BURROUGHS ALSO MIXES GENRES, USES PASTICHE WELL, AND EXPLORES THE INSTABILITY OF THE UNIVERSE. **THEY'RE** NOT AS AMBITIOUS IN AREAS OF GRAMMAR AND SYNTAX AS "THE SOFT MACHINE," ALTHOUGH **THEY'RE** NOT A SIMPLE READ, EITHER. SOME CHARACTERS, FROM DR. BENWAY TO KIM CARSON, SHOW UP IN SEVERAL BOOKS. BURROUGHS CLAIMED:

ALL MY BOOKS ARE ONE BOOK.

IN THE LAST PORTION OF HIS LIFE, BURROUGHS WAS INVOLVED WITH PAINTING, ROCK MUSIC, AND FILM. BURROUGHS'S PAINTING WAS DONE BY BLASTING WITH A SHOTGUN CANS OF PAINT SET IN FRONT OF CANVASES, A TECHNIQUE HE BORROWED FROM OTHERS.

BURROUGHS'S FIRST ART SHOW, IN 1987, SOLD OUT IMMEDIATELY. BY 1989 HE WAS MAKING $3,000 A PAINTING.

BURROUGHS ALSO ACTED IN SEVERAL MOVIES: "THE TWISTER," "IT DON'T PAY TO BE AN HONEST CITIZEN," AND, MOST FAMOUSLY, "DRUGSTORE COWBOY."

BURROUGHS ALSO INFLUENCED FILMMAKERS, INCLUDING MOST PROMINENTLY DAVID CRONEN-BERG, WHO DID A NOTABLY UNSUCCESSFUL ADAPTATION OF "NAKED LUNCH" FOR THE SCREEN.

HIS IMPACT ON ROCK MUSICIANS, AND NOT ONLY PATTI SMITH, IS ALSO PRETTY WELL KNOWN. HE APPEARS ON THE COVER OF THE BEATLES' "SERGEANT PEPPER" ALBUM AND RECORDED WITH LAURIE ANDERSON, KURT COBAIN, THE DISPOSABLE HEROES OF HIPHOPRISY, BILL LASWELL, AND TOM WAITS. THE BANDS STEELY DAN AND THE SOFT MACHINE GOT THEIR NAMES FROM HIS WRITING. DEBORAH HARRY AND LOU REED WERE INTERVIEWED WITH BURROUGHS.

IN FACT HE'S HAD AN INFLUENCE ON SEVERAL ART FORMS, AND IN THAT RESPECT WAS NOT ONLY ONE OF THE MOST IMPORTANT BEATS, BUT ONE OF THE MAJOR, STYLISTICALLY UNIQUE WRITERS TO EMERGE SINCE THE SECOND WORLD WAR.

BURROUGHS DIED IN AUGUST 1997.

94

THE BEATS:
PERSPECTIVES

THE SAN FRANCISCO POETRY RENAISSANCE

THERE WAS A FLOWERING OF POETRY IN THE SAN FRANCISCO AREA DURING THE 1950'S THAT IS OFTEN CONSIDERED PART OF THE BEAT MOVEMENT, PARTLY BECAUSE JACK KEROUAC AND ALLEN GINSBERG MADE A SPLASH IN THE BAY AREA IN 1955. HOWEVER, THIS "RENAISSANCE" WAS WELL UNDER WAY PRIOR TO 1955 AND WAS ROOTED IN THE BAY AREA, NOT GREENWICH VILLAGE.

A LOT OF PEOPLE CONTRIBUTED TO THIS MOVEMENT, ONE OF THE MOST IMPORTANT BEING A MAN DUBBED ITS GODFATHER, KENNETH REXROTH, WHOSE ACCOMPLISHMENTS ARE MANY AND VARIED, AND WHO HAS YET TO RECEIVE SUFFICIENT CREDIT FOR THEM.

REXROTH WAS BORN IN SOUTH BEND, INDIANA, AND MOVED TO CHICAGO AS AN ADOLESCENT. HE NEVER DID COMPLETE HIGH SCHOOL BUT EDUCATED HIMSELF SO WELL THAT HE WAS A "WALKING ENCYCLOPEDIA."

IN CHICAGO REXROTH'S FIRST GREAT PASSION WAS PAINTING. HE WAS, AS A TEENAGER, A BOHEMIAN, PART OF WHAT WAS CALLED THE SECOND CHICAGO RENAISSANCE. HE HUNG AROUND WITH THE MOST ADVANCED THINKERS IN THE CITY AT SUCH BASTIONS OF FINE SPEECH AS THE DILL PICKLE CLUB AND BUG-HOUSE SQUARE.

HE HOBOED OUT WEST FOR A FEW YEARS, WORKING ON RANCHES AND FARMS, AS AN ATTENDANT IN A PSYCHIATRIC HOSPITAL, AND AS A SHORT-ORDER COOK.

HE WAS DEVELOPING A POLITICAL PHILOSOPHY THEN, AND FOUND HE LIKED ANARCHISM BEST. HE HUNG AROUND WITH THE OLD "WOBBLY" CROWD IN SAN FRANCISCO, WHERE HE SETTLED AND WAS A LABOR ORGANIZER DURING THE 1930'S.

BY THE LATE 1920'S REXROTH WAS WRITING POETRY INFLUENCED BY THE IMAGISTS, E.G., WILLIAM CARLOS WILLIAMS AND EZRA POUND. HE GOT SOME OF HIS POEMS PUBLISHED IN MAGAZINES AND WITHHELD OTHERS FOR LATER PUBLICATION.

HIS POETRY STYLE WAS EVOLVING AS HE BECAME INCREASINGLY KNOWLEDGEABLE. "IN WHAT HOUR" (1940) CONTAINS EVERYTHING FROM AN EMOTIONAL RESPONSE TO THE SACCO-VANZETTI TRIAL TO CALM APPRECIATIONS OF NATURE.

DURING THE SECOND WORLD WAR REXROTH, A CONSCIENTIOUS OBJECTOR, WORKED IN A HOSPITAL. HE CONTINUED TO WORK ON HIS POETRY, TOO.

REXROTH DEVELOPED HIS "NATURAL NUMBER" SYSTEM, WHICH WAS METRICALLY IRREGULAR. HE OFTEN USED 7 TO 9 SYLLABLES A LINE TO EMULATE "THE NATURAL CADENCES OF SPEECH."

HIS STUDY OF GREEK, CHINESE, AND JAPANESE POETRY ALSO MARKED HIS WORK.

THEY KNEW WHAT THEY WERE DOING BACK THEN.

DURING THE 1940'S REXROTH BECAME A MAJOR FIGURE IN THE SAN FRANCISCO ART SCENE. HE WAS PUBLISHING HIS POETRY AND WROTE REGULARLY FOR "THE NATION" AND "THE SATURDAY REVIEW" AS WELL AS LOCAL PUBLICATIONS. HIS IN-FLUENCE ON LOCAL WRITERS IS DEALT WITH IN WILLIAM EVERSON'S "REXROTH: SHAKER AND MAKER."

HAVE YOU SEEN REXROTH'S NEW BOOK?

IN 1946 HE HELPED ESTABLISH SAN FRAN-CISCO'S KPFA RADIO STATION AND **BROADCAST** ON IT FREQUENTLY.

WITH A GROUP CALLED THE ANARCHISTS' CIRCLE, HE HELD MEETINGS AND POETRY READINGS THAT WERE ATTENDED BY AS MANY AS 200 PEOPLE. HE WAS A RE-SPECTED LITERARY TRANSLATOR.

WEEK AFTER WEEK VARIOUS PEOPLE LED DISCUSSIONS. THERE WAS NO CHAIRMAN.

MEANWHILE SAN FRANCISCO WAS BECOMING A POETRY CENTER IN THE 40'S AND 50'S. EVERSON, KENNETH PATCHEN, JACK SPICER, ROBERT DUNCAN, AND PHILIP LAMANTIA HAD BEEN ON THE SCENE FOR A WHILE BUT REXROTH, AS EVERSON'S ESSAY POINTED OUT, WAS THE "SHAKER AND THE MAKER."

GRADUALLY SOME EAST COAST BEATS AND SOME GUYS FROM OREGON CAME OUT TO THE BAY AREA. GINSBERG, KEROUAC, GARY SNYDER, AND PHILIP WHALEN BECAME INTEGRATED INTO THE SCENE. THEIR READINGS GOT A GOOD RESPONSE FROM THE PUBLIC.

THEN THE FAMOUS SIX GALLERY READING TOOK PLACE, WHICH UPSET THE POETRY WORLD.

CARL SOLOMON, I'M WITH YOU.

AND WHO WAS ON HAND TO EMCEE THE SHOW AND GIVE ENCOURAGEMENT TO THE YOUNG GUYS? — YOU GUESSED, KENNETH REXROTH.

MICHAEL McCLURE

ALTHOUGH HIS PLAYS "THE BEARD" AND "JOSEPHINE THE MOUSE SINGER" WON OBIES, IN SAN FRANCISCO READERS WERE MORE CONCERNED WITH MICHAEL McCLURE AS A POET. HE ALSO PERFORMED AT THE FAMOUS 1955 "HOWL" PERFORMANCE.

AN ENVIRONMENTALIST, HE READ "FOR THE DEATH OF 100 WHALES," A POEM REACTING TO AN ARTICLE HE'D SEEN IN "TIME," ABOUT BORED NATO TROOPS IN ICELAND WHO HAD SLAUGHTERED A PACK OF WHALES.

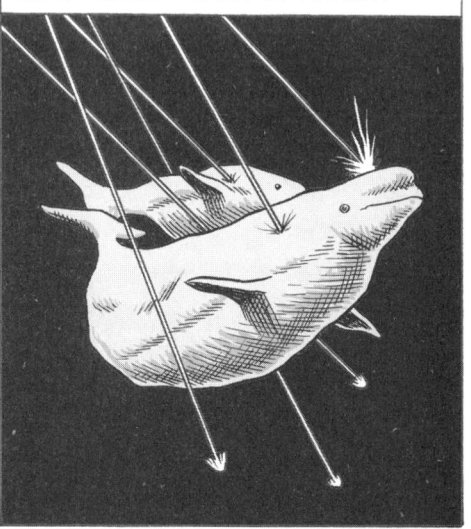

McCLURE WAS VERY INTERESTED IN THE INTERPLAY BETWEEN THE BIOLOGICAL WORLD AND HUMANITY'S SPIRITUAL WORLD.

HE'D BEEN GOING TO COLLEGE IN ARIZONA AND TRYING TO LEARN POETRY ON HIS OWN, BUT WHEN HE MOVED TO THE BAY AREA HE STUDIED WITH AND LEARNED A LOT FROM ROBERT DUNCAN.

AT FIRST HE WROTE ACADEMIC POEMS FOR DUNCAN, THEN BEGAN WRITING THE MODERN STUFF.

HE WAS INTERESTED IN THE WORKS OF THEODORE ROETHKE, DYLAN THOMAS, AND YEATS.

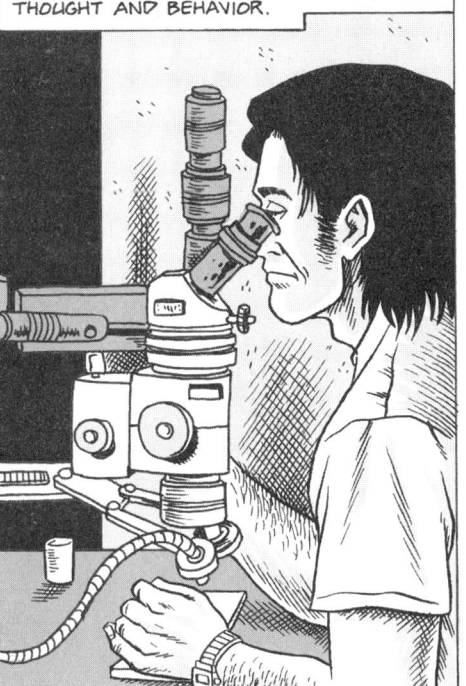

McCLURE TURNED TO SCIENCE, PARTICULARLY BIOLOGY, FOR ENLIGHTENMENT INTO HUMAN THOUGHT AND BEHAVIOR.

BEGINNING IN 1959 HE WROTE PLAYS. THEY HAD POPULAR APPEAL, AND SOON HE FOUND HIMSELF ONE OF THE WEST COAST'S MOST RESPECTED WRITERS.

PHILIP WHALEN

ALSO RECITING POETRY AT GINSBERG'S "HOWL" DEBUT IN SAN FRANCISCO WAS PHILIP WHALEN, GARY SNYDER'S OLD BUDDY FROM REED COLLEGE, AND AN AIR FORCE VETERAN.

HE CAME TO BELIEVE RATHER LATE IN LIFE THAT HE WANTED TO DEVOTE A WHOLE LOT OF TIME TO POETRY. HE WAS OLDER THAN SNYDER AND HAD GOTTEN INTO BUDDHISM EARLIER, SO HE TAUGHT SNYDER QUITE A BIT ABOUT IT.

AFTER GETTING OUT OF THE AIR FORCE, WHALEN DRIFTED AROUND FOR A TIME, TAKING JUST ABOUT ANY JOB HE COULD GET. IN 1957 HE HOOKED UP WITH AN OLD BUDDY WHO'D TURNED POLITICIAN AND KEPT HIM GOING FOR A WHILE.

WHALEN HAD STARTED WRITING POETRY IN COLLEGE, AND SOME OF IT IMPRESSED SOMEBODY, BECAUSE LeROI JONES ASKED HIM FOR A MANUSCRIPT AND PUBLISHED IT AS "LIKE I SAY." IT WAS ENOUGH OF A HIT FOR WHALEN TO SUPPORT HIMSELF BY GOING TO COLLEGE, GIVING READINGS AND CONDUCTING SEMINARS.

LET ME SEE WHAT YOU'VE GOT.

SNYDER SENT FOR WHALEN TO TAKE A JOB TEACHING IN KYOTO. HE WENT THERE AND LOVED IT.

WHALEN BRIEFLY LEFT JAPAN, ONLY TO RETURN IN 1968 AND BEGIN STUDYING BUDDHISM SERIOUSLY. HE HAD SOME BAD LUCK AND HAD TO GO HOME, THOUGH.

SAYONARA!

THEN HE GOT SOME GOOD LUCK AND RE-TURNED TO JAPAN TO STUDY AS A BUDDHIST MONK. HE WAS ORDAINED IN 1973.

IN THE EARLY 1990'S HE HAD HEART TROUBLE AND WAS GOING BLIND, SO HE CAME BACK TO THE STATES. SINCE THEN HE HAS NOT HAD AN IN-DEPENDENT LIFE.

BUT LISTEN, WHALEN IS ONE OF THE FUNNIEST POETS I'VE EVER READ. HE'S GOT A NATURAL COMIC SENSE, WHICH HE DISPLAYS IN INTERVIEWS.

SO I TOLD THE GUY...

HIS CONTRIBUTION TO THE GINSBERG ET AL. READING IN 1955 WAS "PLUS ÇA CHANGE," ABOUT TWO PEOPLE WHO TURNED INTO PARAKEETS.

YOU HAVE TO GO A LONG WAY TO FIND A POET WHO IS AS QUICK AND INFORMAL AS WHALEN. NOT TOO MANY POETS CAN MAKE YOU LAUGH OUT LOUD. HE SHOULD BE BROUGHT MORE TO THE PUBLIC'S ATTENTION.

106

BETWEEN REXROTH AND GARY SNYDER IN THE BAY AREA

NOW, THE BAY AREA HAD BEEN PRODUCING FINE POETS FOR YEARS BEFORE THE LABEL "SAN FRANCISCO POETRY RENAISSANCE" WAS USED.

YOU SHOULD KNOW ABOUT SOME OF THEM SO YOU CAN HAVE A MORE COMPLETE PICTURE OF WHAT THE SCENE WAS LIKE OUT THERE.

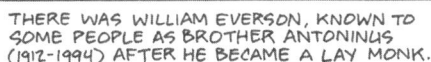

THERE WAS WILLIAM EVERSON, KNOWN TO SOME PEOPLE AS BROTHER ANTONINUS (1912-1994) AFTER HE BECAME A LAY MONK.

HIS FIRST BIG INFLUENCE WAS ROBINSON JEFFERS (1887-1962).

A MAJOR THEME WITH JEFFERS WAS THE INSIGNIFICANCE OF HUMANS COMPARED TO NATURE.

EVERSON'S EARLY WORK GOT HIM LABELED A "NATURE POET," BUT ONE COMMENTATOR HAS REMARKED THAT HIS THEME WAS "VIOLENCE AND MEN'S SUSCEPTIBILITY TO IT," I.E., HIS WORK WAS NOT PASTORAL OR IDYLLIC.

DURING THE SECOND WORLD WAR EVERSON WAS A C.O. IN AN OREGON CAMP WHERE HE WORKED AS A PRINTER.

DURING THE WAR HE MET REXROTH, WHO PROMOTED HIS WORK.

IN 1948 EVERSON HAD "AN INTENSE EMO-TIONAL EXPERIENCE" WHICH LED TO HIS BE-COMING A DOMINICAN MONK, BUT HE STILL WROTE POETRY.

PARTLY DUE TO REXROTH'S PUBLICIZING HIM, EVERSON GAINED NATIONAL ATTENTION.

HOWEVER, HE LEFT THE CHURCH IN 1969 TO GET MARRIED.

FOR A WHILE IN THE LATE 1950'S AND 60'S, EVERSON'S WORK SEEMED TO REFLECT INNER CONFLICT, BUT HIS LATER WRITING SHOWS A CALMER ATTITUDE, PROBABLY BROUGHT ABOUT TO SOME EXTENT BY HIS MARRIAGE.

ROBERT DUNCAN

ROBERT DUNCAN (1919-1988) WAS LONG RE-SPECTED AS ONE OF THE NATION'S FINEST AND MOST ORIGINAL POETS.

HE WAS PUT UP FOR ADOPTION BY A DAY LABORER AND RAISED BY AN UPPER-MIDDLE-CLASS FAMILY WHOSE COMMIT-MENT TO THEOSOPHY INFLUENCED HIM.

HE WENT TO COLLEGE AT U.C. BERKELEY, WHERE SOME OF HIS EARLIEST POEMS WERE PUBLISHED.

AS A 20-YEAR-OLD HE MOVED TO NEW YORK AND MINGLED WITH AN AVANT-GARDE THAT INCLUDED HENRY MILLER, ANAIS NIN, AND SANDERS RUSSELL, WITH WHOM HE EDITED " THE EXPERIMENTAL REVIEW" (1938-40).

DUNCAN'S EMERGING HOMOSEXUALITY CAUSED HIM TO WRITE A COURAGEOUS ESSAY, "THE HOMOSEXUAL IN SOCIETY" (1944), WHICH IN THE SHORT RUN COST HIM DEARLY.

BY 1945 DUNCAN WAS BACK IN CALIFORNIA AND WRITING SOME OF THE BEST POETRY OF HIS EARLY CAREER. HE WAS ASSOCIATED THEN WITH REXROTH.

1954-56 SAW DUNCAN TEACHING AT THE AVANT-GARDE BLACK MOUNTAIN COLLEGE. ITS PRESIDENT, CHARLES OLSON, IN-FLUENCED HIM IN THE AREAS OF PRO-JECTIVE VERSE AND "FIELD" POETRY.

ALL HIS INFLUENCES HAD MESHED BY 1960 WHEN HE BEGAN TO WRITE A SERIES OF BOOKS, "THE OPENING OF THE FIELD," "ROOTS AND BRANCHES" (1964), AND "BENDING THE BOW" (1968), WHICH SECURED HIS REPUTATION AS ONE OF AMERICA'S FINEST POETS.

LAWRENCE FERLINGHETTI

POETRY AND LAWRENCE FERLINGHETTI (1919-) HAVE DONE VERY WELL FOR EACH OTHER. FERLINGHETTI HIMSELF HAS BEEN CITED AS THE BEST-SELLING POET OF THE 20th CENTURY, AND HE'S ALSO BEEN A VERY SUCCESSFUL PUBLISHER AND SELLER OF POETRY BOOKS.

HIS LIFE BEGAN HORRIBLY, HOWEVER. HIS FATHER DIED BEFORE LAWRENCE WAS BORN, AND HIS MOTHER HAD A **POSTPARTUM** NERVOUS BREAKDOWN. HOWEVER, HE CAME UNDER THE CARE OF A WEALTHY FAMILY WHO SAW TO IT THAT HE HAD A FINE EDUCATION.

FERLINGHETTI RECEIVED HIS BA AT COLUMBIA AND HIS DOCTORATE AT THE UNIVERSITY OF PARIS IN 1951, THEN MOVED DIRECTLY TO SAN FRANCISCO.

AFTER TEACHING LANGUAGES AND DOING FREELANCE WRITING, FERLINGHETTI AND HIS PARTNER PETER D. MARTIN ESTABLISHED CITY LIGHTS BOOKSTORE, WHICH SOON BECAME POPULAR WITH SAN FRANCISCO BOHEMIANS.

CITY LIGHTS Booksellers & Pu

POCKET · BOOK · SHOP.

IN 1955 FERLINGHETTI ESTABLISHED HIS OWN POETRY PUBLICATION, ALSO NAMED "CITY LIGHTS," AND PRINTED THE WORKS OF MANY EXCELLENT POETS, INCLUDING HIMSELF.

THE POCKET POETS SERIES

PICTURES
of the gone world

LAWRENCE FERLINGHETTI

NUMBER ONE

HIS WORK WAS OFTEN WITTY AND POIGNANT, SOMETHING THAT IS FREQUENTLY FORGOTTEN DUE TO HIS ENTREPRENEURIAL SUCCESS.

FERLINGHETTI PUBLISHED GINSBERG'S "HOWL," WHICH BROUGHT THE CENSORS DOWN ON HIM, BUT HE WAS ULTIMATELY SUCCESSFUL IN COURT, LEADING TO MORE ANTI-CENSORSHIP TRIALS AND VICTORIES FOR THE PUBLISHER AND HIS AUTHORS.

I WISH ONLY TO SAY THAT THE BOOK IS A THOROUGHLY SERIOUS WORK OF LITERARY ART.

LIKE REXROTH, FERLINGHETTI WAS A FINE POET, BUT FURTHERED THE ART IN OTHER WAYS AS WELL.

GREGORY CORSO

NEXT TO ALLEN GINSBERG, GREGORY CORSO WAS PROBABLY THE MOST POPULAR OF THE EAST COAST BEAT POETS.

HE LED A CHECKERED EXISTENCE. ABANDONED BY HIS FAMILY, HE WAS ON HIS OWN IN NEW YORK'S LITTLE ITALY AT 12, WHEN HE INITIALLY GOT BUSTED.

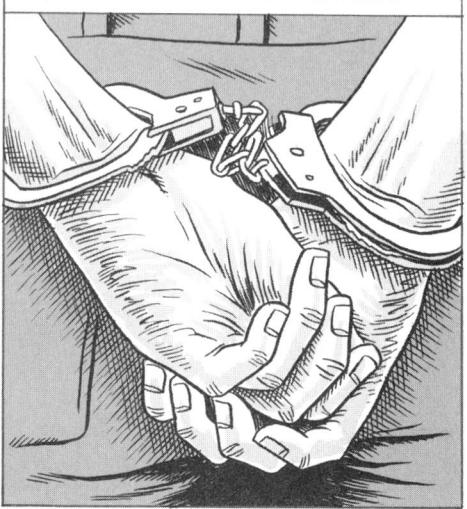

AT 16 HE WAS SENT TO JAIL AGAIN FOR THEFT, THIS TIME FOR THREE YEARS.

THERE HE BECAME AN AUTODIDACT, VORACIOUSLY CONSUMING THE PRISON LIBRARY'S STACK OF BOOKS. HE IMMERSED HIMSELF IN THE CLASSICS.

IN 1950 HE MET GINSBERG, WHO HIPPED HIM TO MODERNIST POETRY, WHICH HE EVENTUALLY WROTE HIMSELF.

CORSO'S POETRY HAS BEEN CALLED UNEVEN, BUT AT HIS BEST HE IS MIGHTY GOOD — WITTY, COMPASSIONATE, AND CLEVER.

IN 1954 HE SETTLED IN BOSTON, WHERE HE AGAIN WENT ON A READING BINGE, AT THE HARVARD LIBRARY. THE STUDENTS THERE DUG HIM AND FINANCED HIS FIRST POETRY VOLUME,"THE VESTAL LADY ON BRATTLE AND OTHER POEMS."

HE PUBLISHED RATHER IRREGULARLY AFTER THAT, BUT SOME OF HIS WORK WAS HIGHLY PRAISED. HE STILL HAS A GROUP OF AVID ADMIRERS, INCLUDING PATTI SMITH, WHO WROTE THE FOREWORD FOR "THE SELECTED LETTERS OF GREGORY CORSO."

LEROI JONES/AMIRI BARAKA

LeROI JONES (1934–) WAS ONE OF THE MOST PROMINENT OF THE **SECOND** GENERATION OF BEATS. HE WENT THROUGH A PERIOD OF BLACK NATIONALISM, WHEN HE CHANGED HIS NAME TO AMIRI BARAKA, AND HE **LATER** ADOPTED MARXISM AND BECAME A SPOKESMAN FOR OPPRESSED THIRD WORLD NATIONS.

HE WAS BORN IN NEWARK, NEW JERSEY, WENT TO RUTGERS, HARVARD, AND COLUMBIA UNIVERSITIES, AND SPENT 3 YEARS IN THE AIR FORCE. WHEN HE RETURNED TO NEW YORK HE LIVED IN GREENWICH VILLAGE AS A BOHEMIAN, WRITING POETRY AND EDITING OR CO-EDITING A COUPLE OF AVANT-GARDE PUBLICATIONS—"YUGEN" (WITH HETTIE JONES) AND "FLOATING BEAR" (WITH DIANE DI PRIMA). AT THAT TIME HIS WRITING WAS INFLUENCED BY CHARLES OLSON AND ALLEN GINSBERG.

HIS FIRST BOOK OF POETRY, "PREFACE TO A TWENTY VOLUME SUICIDE," CAUSED AN OBSERVER TO NOTE THAT WHILE BARAKA'S WORK WAS FULL OF ALLUSIONS TO BLACK CULTURE...

WITH THE RISE OF THE CIVIL RIGHTS MOVEMENT AND THIRD-WORLD ASPIRATIONS, BARAKA ADOPTED A BLACK NATIONALIST POSITION, EXPRESSED IN HIS PRIZE-WINNING PLAY "DUTCHMAN" (1964).

YOU AIN'T NO NIGGER! YOU'RE JUST A DIRTY WHITE MAN.

WHEN MALCOLM X WAS MURDERED IN 1965, BARAKA MOVED TO HARLEM AND FOUNDED THE BLACK ARTS REPERTORY THEATRE SCHOOL THERE.

HOWEVER, IN 1974 BARAKA CAME TO SEE BLACK NATIONALISM IN NEGATIVE TERMS AND DENOUNCED IT AS RACIST.

IN 1974 HE ALSO BEGAN WRITING MARXIST-INFLUENCED POEMS AND PLAYS AND CALLING FOR THE ESTABLISHMENT OF SOCIALIST STATES.

NOW IN HIS SEVENTIES, BARAKA REMAINS CONTROVERSIAL, BUT SEEMS TO BE WELL ON HIS WAY TOWARD ACCEPTANCE BY THE ACADEMIC AND CRITICAL ESTABLISHMENT.

LeRoi Jones
1934 —
Amiri Baraka
1934

CHARLES OLSON

ALTHOUGH NOT GENERALLY THOUGHT OF AS BEAT POETS, CHARLES OLSON AND ROBERT CREELEY HAD FREQUENT AND CLOSE RELATIONS WITH THE BEATS.

OLSON (1910-1970), ONE OF THE MAJOR 20TH-CENTURY POETRY THEORISTS, WAS BORN IN WORCESTER, MASSACHUSETTS. HE WAS A PHI BETA KAPPA KNOWN FOR HIS ESSAYS ON HERMAN MELVILLE, BUT AFTER WORKING IN POLITICS DURING THE 1940'S, OLSON TURNED TO POETRY, BECOMING RECTOR AT THE REVOLUTIONARY BLACK MOUNTAIN COLLEGE IN NORTH CAROLINA.

HE IS PERHAPS MOST WELL-KNOWN FOR HIS ESSAY AND THEORY REGARDING "PROJECTIVE VERSE." HE DEFINES THE ROLE OF THE SYLLABLE AND LINE PRECISELY IN THIS WORK.

PROJECTIVE VERSE BY CHARLES OLSON

OLSON, INFLUENCED BY EZRA POUND AND WILLIAM CARLOS WILLIAMS, IN TURN INFLUENCED MANY POETS, INCLUDING CREELEY AND ROBERT DUNCAN.

CHARLES OLSON'S COLLECTED POEMS.

OLSON'S MAJOR POETIC WORK WAS "THE MAXIMUS POEMS", PUBLISHED IN 3 VOLUMES. IT HAS BEEN DESCRIBED AS "MAXIMUS LABORS TO FOUND IN GLOUCESTER, MASSACHUSETTS, A COMMUNITY DEVOTED TO CREATIVE PURSUITS. ITS MEMBERS WILL BE THE READERS OF THE POEMS, TO WHOM MAXIMUS HOPES TO TRANSFER THE SAME CREATIVE ENERGY WHICH MOTIVATES HIM." HIS EFFORTS ARE SABOTAGED BY CAPITALISM, BUT HE CONTINUES TO WRITE AND MAKE A GREAT EFFORT TO REALIZE HIS AMBITIONS.

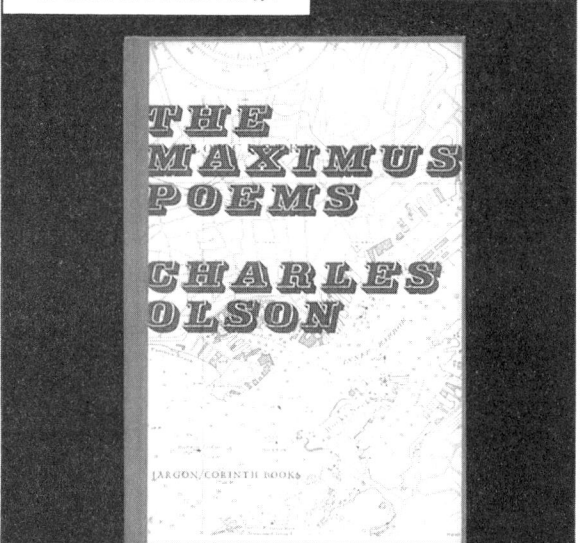

OLSON STAYED AT BLACK MOUNTAIN COLLEGE FROM 1951 UNTIL 1956, WHEN ECONOMIC PROBLEMS CAUSED ITS SHUTDOWN. ONE OF THE MOST PROGRESSIVE COLLEGES ANYWHERE, IT NUMBERED AMONG ITS FACULTY JOHN CAGE.

LATER, OLSON TAUGHT AT THE STATE UNIVERSITY OF NEW YORK IN BUFFALO AND THE UNIVERSITY OF CONNECTICUT.

UNFORTUNATELY, HIS LIFE WAS CUT SHORT BY ILLNESS IN 1970, BUT BY THAT TIME HE HAD ESTABLISHED HIMSELF AS ONE OF THE MAJOR POETS OF THE SECOND HALF OF THE 20TH CENTURY.

ROBERT CREELEY

THE WORK OF ROBERT CREELEY (1926-2005) IS CHARACTERIZED BY ITS IMPROVISATORY QUALITY.

HE WAS BORN IN ARLINGTON, MASSACHUSETTS, AND TAUGHT AT BLACK MOUNTAIN COLLEGE IN 1954-1955. AFTER IT CLOSED HE TAUGHT AT A BOYS' SCHOOL IN ALBUQUERQUE, NEW MEXICO. HE RECEIVED NATIONAL ATTENTION FOR HIS COLLECTION "FOR LOVE: POEMS 1950-1960."

FORM IS NEVER MORE THAN AN EXTENSION OF CONTENT.

HIS WORK WAS KNOWN FOR ITS ECONOMY. A CRITIC OBSERVED,

CREELEY HAS SHAPED HIS OWN AUDIENCE. THE MUCH-IMITATED, OFTEN DILUTED MINIMALISM, THE EXPRESSION OF EMOTION INTO VERSE IN WHICH SCARCELY A SYLLABLE IS WASTED, HAS DECISIVELY MARKED A GENERATION OF POETS.

ANOTHER COMMENTATOR NOTED,

CREELEY SPEAKS OF WORDS AS THE ABSTRACT EXPRESSIONIST PAINTERS SPOKE OF PAINT. THE POEMS ARE, AS IT WERE, EVENTS, PHYSIOLOGICAL EVENTS, MOVEMENTS.

IN "HELLO: A JOURNAL, FEBRUARY 29–MAY 3, 1976," CREELEY CONSIDERS THE POSSIBILITY OF USING MEMORY INSTEAD OF THE PRESENT AS A SOURCE FOR HIS WRITING.

IN "LATER" (1979), CREELEY EMPHASIZES MEMORY EVEN MORE. A COMMENTATOR, IN "THE NEW YORK TIMES BOOK REVIEW" WROTE:

IN GENERAL THE STRONGER THE NOTE OF ELEGIAC BAFFLE-MENT AND RAGE (THE PAST UTTERLY GONE, THE COMPENSATING WISDOM NOT FORTHCOMING), THE BETTER THE WRITING. THAT IS, PEOPLE GROW OLDER BUT LEARN LITTLE.

AS TIME WENT ON, MORE AND MORE OF CREELEY'S WRITING WAS FILTERED THROUGH MEMORY.

I WRITE TO REALIZE THE WORLD AS ONE HAS COME TO LIVE IN IT, THUS TO GIVE TESTAMENT. I WRITE TO MOVE IN WORDS, A HUMAN DELIGHT. I WRITE WHEN NO OTHER ACT IS POSSIBLE.

121

FROM THE BEGINNING, SAN FRANCISCO WAS A MAGNET FOR THE ADVENTUROUS AND FREETHINKING WRITER.

RICHARD HENRY DANA, WHO SAILED TO S.F. BAY IN THE 1830'S, DETAILED THE ABUSE OF ORDINARY SAILORS BY SHIPS' OFFICERS IN *TWO YEARS BEFORE THE MAST*.

THIRTY YEARS LATER, MARK TWAIN, A LATE-LIFE SOCIALIST (& LIFELONG SOCIAL CRITIC) WROTE FOR THE *MORNING CALL* (WHICH DIDN'T ALWAYS APPRECIATE HIS COLUMNS THAT EXPOSED POLITICAL CORRUPTION AND ANTI-CHINESE BIAS).

DAMNATION! THEY'VE CUT ANOTHER OF MY EXPOSÉS OF POLICE BRUTALITY!

HENRY GEORGE, "THE PROPHET OF SAN FRANCISCO," PROPOSED HIS REVOLUTIONARY IDEA OF THE SINGLE TAX.

CHARLOTTE PERKINS GILMAN, SOCIALIST & FEMINIST, ORGANIZED CALIFORNIA WOMEN'S CONGRESSES BEFORE RETURNING EAST TO WRITE *HERLAND*, A UTOPIAN NOVEL.

THE MAN WITH THE HOE
BY EDWIN MARKHAM

BY REASON OF UNIVERSAL DEMAND.

IN MY UTOPIA, MEN AND WOMEN ARE EQUAL!

HERLAND

EDWARD MARKHAM WROTE A POEM HEARD 'ROUND THE WORLD, "THE MAN WITH THE HOE," A RALLYING CRY FOR THE POOR AND EXPLOITED.

JACK LONDON EDUCATED HIMSELF IN THE OAKLAND PUBLIC LIBRARY, AND WORKED AS A LABORER, SEALER, AND OYSTER PIRATE BEFORE BECOMING A WORLDWIDE BESTSELLING AUTHOR.

FRANK NORRIS'S NOVELS EXPOSED THE GREED OF AMERICAN MONOPOLIES AND MARKETS.

I WOULD RATHER BE ASHES THAN DUST!

BY GOD, I TOLD THEM THE TRUTH!

THE OCTOPUS

NORTH BEACH BECAME A BOHEMIA OF ARTISTS' AND WRITERS' STUDIOS.

WILLIAM SAROYAN, AN ARMENIAN-AMERICAN, WROTE EXUBERANT PLAYS AND STORIES ABOUT THE IMMIGRANT EXPERIENCE.

THE DETECTIVE NOIR MASTER DASHIELL HAMMETT SET HIS STORIES IN SAN FRANCISCO'S GRITTY UNDERBELLY.

OTHER INSURGENT WRITERS MADE THEIR MARK IN S.F. OVER THE EARLY YEARS: AMBROSE BIERCE, JOHN STEINBECK, IRVING STONE, EMMA GOLDMAN, MARGARET ANDERSON, AND HENRY MILLER.

CLASS STRUGGLE WAS A CONSTANT. RANK-AND-FILE JOURNALIST MIKE QUIN WROTE A DRAMATIC AND SYMPATHETIC ACCOUNT OF THE DOCKWORKERS' STRUGGLE IN *THE BIG STRIKE*.

ACCORDING TO QUIN:

"The laboring population laid down its tools in a General Strike. An uncanny quiet settled over the acres of buildings. The dirt of commercial activity gave way to the murmur of voices in the streets. . . . There were no bombs. There were no rioting mobs. These existed only in the daily press . . ."

BITS HAYDEN'S WOOD ENGRAVING OF THE S.F. GENERAL STRIKE, 1934.

THE ORGANIZED HORRORS OF WORLD WAR II AND THE THREAT OF NUCLEAR WARFARE INSPIRED A MOOD OF PACIFISM AND ANARCHISM IN THE BAY AREA.

FROM *THE ARK*:

". . . Present-day society which is becoming more and more subject to the State with its many forms of corrupt power and oppression, has become the real enemy of individual liberty. . . ."

BETWEEN 1944 AND 1948, *CIRCLE* MAGAZINE PUBLISHED ANTIWAR, ANARCHIST, AND ANTI-AUTHORITARIAN VIEWPOINTS, TOGETHER WITH EXPERIMENTATION IN THE ARTS.

IN 1947, A MORE MILITANT SISTER MAGAZINE WAS BORN: SAN FRANCISCO'S *THE ARK*.

IN 1949, *KPFA*, THE FIRST LISTENER-SPONSORED RADIO STATION, WAS LAUNCHED IN BERKELEY. IT WAS AN INTELLECTUAL "FREE SPACE" THEN UNKNOWN ON AMERICAN RADIO WAVES, BROADCASTING GREAT POETRY AND LITERATURE, POLITICAL COMMENTARY, JAZZ AND CLASSICAL MUSIC, AND CULTURAL NEWS.

THIS WAS THE BIRTH OF PACIFICA RADIO.

HIPSTERS BEGAN HITCHHIKING, CATCHING FREIGHTS, AND DRIVING FROM COAST TO COAST. THEY GATHERED IN SAN FRANCISCO, WHERE JAZZ CLUBS FLOURISHED AND RACIAL BARRIERS WERE BEING UNDERMINED BY THE BOHEMIAN COUNTERCULTURE.

ONE NIGHT WHEN SOME JAZZ MUSICIANS WERE IMPROVISING AT THE CELLAR, RUTH WEISS JOINED IN WITH A POEM. EVERYONE LOVED IT, AND WEDNESDAY BECAME POETRY & JAZZ NIGHT.

HERE'S A POEM FOR YOU!

THE POET BOB KAUFMAN WAS A GREAT JAZZ AFICIONADO, AND HIS POETRY SHARED WITH BEBOP ITS SHIFTING TEMPOS, RHYTHMS, AND IMPROVISATIONS.

MICHAEL McCLURE

PHILIP LAMANTIA

JOHN WIENERS

DAVID MELTZER

WRITERS FROM THE EAST (GINSBERG, KEROUAC, FERLINGHETTI, DI PRIMA, WIENERS, MELTZER) JOINED FORCES WITH THE WESTERNERS (SNYDER, McCLURE, REXROTH, LAMANTIA, DUNCAN, KYGER, WHALEN, WEISS, PATCHEN) AND THE BEAT GENERATION IGNITED.

ONE DAY IN 1953, RETURNING FROM HIS PAINTING STUDIO, LAWRENCE FERLINGHETTI SAW A SIGN ON COLUMBUS AVENUE. PETER D. MARTIN, SON OF THE ANARCHIST CARLO TRESCA, AND EDITOR OF THE POP-CULTURE MAGAZINE *CITY LIGHTS*, HAD DECIDED TO DO SOMETHING NEW.

POCKET BOOK STORE OPENING SOON

I'VE ALWAYS WANTED A BOOKSTORE! DO YOU WANT A PARTNER?

OK, WE'LL EACH INVEST $500! THAT WILL BE A GOOD START!

MARTIN WENT TO NEW YORK IN 1955, AND SHIG MURAO BEGAN MANAGING THE STORE. MURAO WAS A NISEI, A SECOND-GENERATION JAPANESE-AMERICAN, WHO WAS SENT WITH HIS FAMILY TO A "RELOCATION" CAMP IN MINIDOKA, IDAHO, DURING WORLD WAR II.

AFTER THE WAR, MURAO CAME TO SAN FRANCISCO AND BECAME AN IMPOSING AND ERUDITE PRESENCE AT CITY LIGHTS BOOKSTORE.

FERLINGHETTI BEGAN CITY LIGHTS PUBLICATIONS WITH A BOOK OF HIS OWN POEMS, *PICTURES OF THE GONE WORLD*.

IN PARIS, AFTER THE WAR, BOOKSTORES WERE PUBLISHING BOOKS, TOO. THAT'S WHAT I WANT TO DO.

I NEVER WANTED TO PUBLISH JUST THE BEATS, BUT WANTED NEW VOICES FROM AROUND THE WORLD. BY 1961, WE HAD 26 TITLES ON OUR LIST, 13 OF THEM IN THE POCKET POETS SERIES.

BANNED BOOKS

IN 1957, FERLINGHETTI WAS ARRESTED FOR SELLING GINSBERG'S *HOWL*, TRIED IN S.F. MUNICIPAL COURT, AND, AFTER A LONG TRIAL, ACQUITTED.

THE POCKET POETS SERIES

HOWL
AND OTHER POEMS
ALLEN GINSBERG
Introduction by
William Carlos Williams

NUMBER FOUR

THIS WORK HAS REDEEMING SOCIAL VALUE!

JUDGE CLAYTON HORN

128

THE BEATS REVOLUTIONIZED AMERICAN CULTURE AND CONSCIOUSNESS. THEY DEMOCRATIZED POETRY, REVIVING THE ORAL TRADITION, TAKING POETRY OUT OF THE ACADEMY AND INTO THE STREETS.

JACK KEROUAC

I DEMAND THAT THE HUMAN RACE CEASE MULTIPLYING ITS KIND AND BOW OUT I ADVISE IT.

THE BEATS CHALLENGED THE SEXUAL AND POLITICAL VALUES OF THE 1950S, OPENING THE DOOR TO WRITERS WHO WERE FEMALE, GAY & LESBIAN, AND FROM ETHNIC MINORITIES.

OH LOST MOON SISTERS / CRESCENT IN HAIR, SEA UNDERFOOT DO YOU WANDER . . .

DIANE DI PRIMA

WHAT CAN I SAY? / IT IS BETTER TO HAVED LOVED AND LOST / THAN TO PUT LINOLEUM IN YOUR LIVING ROOMS?

LEROI JONES

NANCY J. PETERS JOINED CITY LIGHTS BOOKS IN 1971, TAKING ON TOP PUBLISHING AND MANAGEMENT ROLES OVER THE YEARS.

SINCE IT BEGAN, CITY LIGHTS HAS PUBLISHED THE BEATS AND MANY OTHER VISIONARY WRITERS AND RADICAL THINKERS.

THE BOOKSTORE SPECIALIZES IN LITERATURE, THE ARTS, AND PROGRESSIVE POLITICAL ANALYSIS.

WE OFFER THE BEST BOOKS FROM UNIVERSITY PRESSES AND THE INDEPENDENTS,

AND WE STOCK LOTS OF POETRY AND HARD-TO-FIND BOOKS FROM SMALL PRESS PUBLISHERS.

IN THE EARLY '80S, PAUL YAMAZAKI BECAME THE CHIEF BOOK BUYER. YAMAZAKI, A JAPANESE-AMERICAN, ALSO SPENT TIME AS AN INFANT IN A "RELOCATION CAMP" WITH HIS MOTHER & SISTER, WHILE HIS FATHER SERVED IN THE U.S. ARMY.

LET'S GET MORE GRAPHIC NOVELS AND ZINES!

I'M GOING TO ORDER MORE BOOKS ON CENTRAL ASIA AND THE MIDDLE EAST!

WE NEED TO EXPAND THE MUCKRAKING SECTION!

130

AFTER 9/11, WHEN THE BUSH ADMINISTRATION WAS GIVEN CARTE BLANCHE, WITHOUT DEBATE, BANNERS READING "DISSENT IS NOT UN-AMERICAN" WERE DISPLAYED ON THE FRONT OF THE BOOKSTORE, IN COLLABORATION WITH THE S.F. PRINT COLLECTIVE.

IN 2001, CITY LIGHTS BECAME AN OFFICIAL HISTORIC LANDMARK "FOR ITS SEMINAL ROLE IN THE LITERARY AND CULTURAL DEVELOPMENT OF SAN FRANCISCO, FOR CHAMPIONING FIRST AMENDMENT RIGHTS, AND FOR GIVING VOICE TO WRITERS EVERYWHERE."

City Lights Booksellers & Publishers
REGISTERED LANDMARK
No. 228
CITY & COUNTY OF SAN FRANCISCO

TODAY, CITY LIGHTS HAS COME TO SYMBOLIZE THE AMERICAN SPIRIT OF FREE INTELLECTUAL INQUIRY.

Kenneth Patchen

MY HIGH SCHOOL FRIEND DAVE BURTON TURNED ME ON TO KENNETH PATCHEN'S PICTURE POEMS IN 1961.

THIS STUFF IS FANTASTIC. BUT ARE YOU ALLOWED TO PUT CREATURES IN POEMS?

LUMBER-JACKET

WE WERE ON THE LOOKOUT FOR ANYTHING "BEAT," WHICH FOR US MEANT TOUGH, FUNNY, PISSED-OFF & ECSTATIC. PATCHEN HAD IT ALL!

KENNETH PATCHEN WAS BORN IN 1911 TO A YOUNGSTOWN STEELWORKER. HE CREDITED HIS SCOTS GRANDFATHER, WHO SHARED HIS BEDROOM AND RECITED ROBERT BURNS POEMS TO HIM AS A CHILD, WITH INSPIRING HIM TO WRITE.

Is there a bard of rustic song,
Who, noteless, steals the crowds among,
That weekly this area throng,
    O pass not by!
But with a frater-
    feeling strong,
Here, heave
    a sigh!

AFTER A YEAR OF COLLEGE DURING THE DEPRESSION, PATCHEN WENT ON THE ROAD WORKING AT ANY JOB HE COULD FIND.

I remember you could put daisies
On the windowsill at night and in
The morning they'd be covered
      with soot
You couldn't tell what they
      were anymore.
A hell of a fat chance my orange
      bears had!

HIS EARLY WORK MARKED HIM AS A REVOLUTIONIST — IN THE LINGO OF THAT TIME, A "PROLETARIAN POET."

Every man's at war who's hungry
and hunted whether in Omaha or Tokyo

Here they come look out they
mean business they mean an end
to standing in rain waiting for
freights out of Toledo or Detroit

133

HE MARRIED MIRIAM OKEMUS, THE DAUGHTER OF A FINNISH-AMERICAN RADICAL FAMILY, IN 1934.

She knows it's raining and my room is warm

But she is proud and beautiful and I have no money

IN 1937 THEY MOVED TO HOLLYWOOD, WHERE PATCHEN WORKED AS A "SCRIPT DOCTOR."

ONE NIGHT AS HE TRIED TO SEPARATE TWO CARS WITH LOCKED BUMPERS, PATCHEN SUFFERED A RUPTURED DISK THAT PLAGUED HIM THE REST OF HIS LIFE.

There was a tame streetcar conductor
Who one day was considerably surprised
To have it suddenly
bite his behind

JUST DRIVE AHEAD WHILE I RAISE THIS ONE UP—

OOPS

IN 1938 HE MET JAMES LAUGHLIN OF NEW DIRECTIONS, WHO HIRED HIM AS A SHIPPING CLERK BUT PUBLISHED A GOOD DEAL OF HIS WORK OVER THE YEARS AS WELL.

Our supper is plain but we are very wonderful.

DURING THE EARLY 1950s PATCHEN MOVED TO SAN FRANCISCO, WHERE HE WAS WELCOMED BY THE EMERGING "SAN FRANCISCO SCENE."

HE WAS HIP BEFORE THERE WAS HIP!

IT'S HIM!

MAESTRO!

OLD PAL!

WOTTA MAN, MAN!

FERLINGHETTI

REXROTH

Not really knowing whether I'm running from somebody or somebody's just chasing me because I'm running

135

PATCHEN BECAME ONE OF THE FIRST POETS TO READ ACCOMPANIED BY JAZZ MUSICIANS, AFTER A 1957 SPINAL FUSION OPERATION RESTORED HIS MOBILITY.

TA-DUM T-DUM TA-DUM TA-DUM T-DUM TDUM TA-DUM, HIS TRUTH IS MARCHING ON...

BAND KICKS OFF WITH MANIC VERSION OF "JOHN BROWN'S BODY"

You know it's a funny thing to realize that you're living inside yourself I mean that you're alone there inside yourself and that in some different sort of way everybody else is living there too—You know a lot of people remind me of that John Brown—They're MOULDERING AWAY allright except the real bad bit is THEY'RE USING THEMSELVES FOR THE GRAVE!

BUT DURING A 1959 DIAGNOSTIC PROCEDURE, A MYSTERIOUS ACCIDENT UNDID THE SPINAL FUSION. PATCHEN WAS BEDRIDDEN THE REST OF HIS LIFE.

WE DROPPED A PATIENT TODAY.

OOPS. ANYBODY IMPORTANT?

JUST A POET.

POLITICALLY & CULTURALLY, PATCHEN WAS A REBEL. THOUGH VARIOUSLY IDENTIFIED AS A COMMUNIST, ANARCHIST, TROTSKYIST, BEAT, SURREALIST, OR DADAIST, HE REJECTED ALL LABELS.

THIS WRITER THINKS I'M A "DADAIST"

OH, BUT THERE ARE PLENTY OF OTHERS.

WE CAN ASSERT OUR BELIEF IN THE ESSENTIAL NOBILITY OF MAN—

STATING THE "DADA" POSITION, HE ASKS "WHAT OTHER HONEST RESPONSE CAN THERE BE TO SOCIETY'S HYPOCRISY THAN A FURIOUS BURST OF LAUGHTER"?

HI-BROW POETRY JOURNAL

OUR HUMILITY BEFORE THE ART OF POETRY ITSELF

ABOVE ALL HE HATED WAR.

Any man with a gun aimed at another man is Hitler

WE CAN WEEP & OUR TEARS WILL NOT BE THOSE OF SPOILED CHILDREN!

PATCHEN WAS AN AMAZING ARTIST WHO WROTE PROSE AND POETRY, DID DRAWINGS, AND USED VARIED TYPEFACES IN HIS WORK, SOMETIMES IN THE SAME PIECE.

(KENNETH IS IN CONSTANT PAIN. THAT'S WHY HE DOES THE PICTURE POEMS— HE CAN FINISH THEM IN A FEW HOURS, WHICH IS ABOUT AS LONG AS HE'S ABLE TO WORK)

We don't want much we want everything

KENNETH, HERE'S THE YOUNG MAN WHO WANTS TO INTERVIEW YOU.

I saw the big shtoonks Kicking the cans off the little shtoonks

AND!... Charging them for the service.

I KNOW YOU'VE BEEN THROUGH SOME ROUGH TIMES—

HOW HAVE YOU MANAGED TO RETAIN YOUR SENSE OF WONDER?

I CANNOT CONCEIVE OF ANY WAY IN WHICH I COULD LOSE THE SENSE OF WONDER. TO ME THAT WOULD BE DEATH.

EVERY TIME PAUL KLEE APPROACHED A CANVAS IT WAS WITH A FEELING OF "WELL, HERE I AM, I KNOW NOTHING ABOUT PAINTING, LET'S LEARN SOMETHING, LET'S FEEL SOMETHING."

THIS IS WHAT DISTINGUISHES THE ARTIST OF THE FIRST RANK—

—ADMITTING THAT NO TRUE SELF-EXPRESSION IS POSSIBLE, YOU'LL HAVE TO TRY IT AGAIN TOMORROW.

There is a kindness of willing & a cruelty of won'ting

138

KENNETH PATCHEN'S HEART GAVE OUT ON JAN. 8, 1972. MIRIAM LATER SAID THAT WHEN HE DIED "HE LOOKED LIKE SOMEONE WHO HAD BEEN HOMELESS FOR 3,000 YEARS."

WRITTEN BY NICK THORKELSON & HARVEY PEKAR. DRAWINGS BY NICK THORKELSON.

SOURCES: MOST INFO IS FROM LARRY SMITH'S BIOGRAPHY, KENNETH PATCHEN: REBEL POET IN AMERICA. GENE DETRO'S 1968 INTERVIEW EXCERPTED ABOVE AND PATCHEN'S COMMENTS ON DADAISM ARE FROM KENNETH PATCHEN: A COLLECTION OF ESSAYS, EDITED BY RICHARD G. MORGAN. BITS OF PATCHEN'S WRITINGS AND DRAWINGS ARE FROM BEFORE THE BRAVE (1936), FIRST WILL AND TESTAMENT (1939), CLOTH OF THE TEMPEST (1943), THE JOURNAL OF ALBION MOONLIGHT (1941), PANELS FOR THE WALLS OF HEAVEN (1946), WHEN WE WERE HERE TOGETHER (1952-57), BUT EVEN SO (1968), HURRAH FOR ANYTHING (1957), BECAUSE IT IS (1960), HALLELUJAH ANYWAY (1966), AND WONDERINGS (1971). POETRY WITH JAZZ IS FROM KENNETH PATCHEN READS WITH JAZZ IN CANADA (FOLKWAYS LP 1959, LOCUST CD 2004). THIS COMIC IS FOR DAVID BRYANT BURTON.

THE POET BEGAN TO DISCOVER HIM- SELF. HE READ VORACIOUSLY. HE WROTE EVERY DAY.

I AM TOUCHED BY THE MARVELOUS, AS THE MERMAID'S NIMBLE FINGERS GO THROUGH MY HAIR.

Vaché

I'M SICK OF WAR AND THE CIVILIZATION THAT CREATES IT!

Breton

LET'S LOOK TO OUR DREAMS AND THE MAGICAL, TO THE CREATIONS OF SO-CALLED PRIMITIVE PEO- PLES FOR NEW INSPIRATIONS.

AT 15, HE WROTE ANDRE BRETON, THEN LIVING IN NY, A REFUGEE FROM YET ANOTHER WAR.

A true revolutionary poet cannot help defying every social and political instrument that has caused death and exploitation. Poetry is the highest principle of language.

BRETON WAS WORKING ON HIS ODE TO THE FRENCH UTOPIAN FOURIER WHEN PHILIP'S POEMS ARRIVED. ACCEPTING POEMS FOR HIS SURREALIST JOURNAL *VVV*, HE WROTE PHILIP...

Yours is a voice that rises once in a hundred years...

LAMANTIA DROPPED OUT OF HIGH SCHOOL, WENT TO NY TO MEET BRETON AND THE SURREALISTS IN EXILE.

OBJECTIVE CHANCE...

AUTOMATISM... ...MAD LOVE..

REVOLUTION!

Tanguy

LAMANTIA ALSO CONTRIBUTED POEMS AND COMMUNICATIONS TO *HEMISPHERES*, *CIRCLE*, *HORIZON*, *RESISTANCE* (NEW YORK), *NOW* (LONDON), AND *VIEW*, OF WHICH HE WAS A CONTRIBUTING EDITOR.

PHILIP, JOHN CAGE, PARKER TYLER, AND ALEXANDER HAMMID STROLL THROUGH MAYA DEREN'S FILM *AT LAND.*

IN NY, PHILIP AND HIS FRIEND THE MUSICOLOGIST AND FILMMAKER HARRY SMITH HAUNTED JAZZ CLUBS TO HEAR CHARLIE PARKER, DIZZY GILLESPIE, AND THELONIUS MONK.

SO WHAT DO YOU THINK, PHILIP?

IT'S POETRY, MAN, SURREALISM TRANSFORMED INTO MUSIC!

IN THE LATE 40'S AND EARLY 50'S, AN EXPLOSIVE RENEWAL OF POETRY SPREAD ACROSS THE COUNTRY.

LAMANTIA HAD ASSOCIATIONS WITH WRITERS AND ARTISTS OF A NEW ALTERNATIVE CULTURE THAT WOULD LATER BE CALLED THE BEAT GENERATION IN NEW YORK (JACK KEROUAC, GREGORY CORSO, ALLEN GINSBERG, JOHN WIENERS, TED JOANS, HOWARD HART) AND IN SF (MICHAEL AND JOANNA McCLURE, KENNETH REXROTH, ROBERT DUNCAN, ROBERT CREELEY, BOB KAUFMAN, JAY DEFEO, BRUCE CONNER, LARRY JORDAN, DAVID MELTZER)

LAMANTIA   WIENERS   McCLURE   MELTZER

AT KENNETH REXROTH'S EVENINGS AT HIS SAN FRANCISCO HOME, INTELLECTUALS, ARTISTS, AND WORKERS GATHERED FOR POETRY AND POLITICAL DEBATE.

BARCELONA IS THE MODEL!

THE ANARCHISTS AND THE POUM HAD THE SUPPORT OF THE LARGE MAJORITY OF THE PEOPLE.

YES, BUT OUR ENEMIES WERE BETTER ARMED!

142

IN 1947, IN SAN FRANCISCO, PHILIP, ROBERT STOCK, AND SANDERS RUSSELL LAUNCHED *THE ARK*, A JOURNAL OF PACIFIST ANARCHIST WRITING.

HERE IT IS! HOT OFF THE MIMEOGRAPH!

YES! YES! YES! LUMINOUS NOW!

THAT BOOK IN YOUR POCKET, *MALDOROR*...IT'S THE GREATEST! CHICAGO, NEW YORK, LOS ANGELES HAVE GONE DOWN.

IT WAS NAILED WHERE THE DOOR HAD BEEN, NOW THE DUNES HAVE LOCKED IT OPEN.

LAMANTIA WAS CAUGHT UP IN THE PROTO-BEAT SUBTERRANEAN SCENE. JOHN HOFFMAN, POET AND HIPSTER, WAS HIS BEST FRIEND.

KEROUAC WAS IN LOVE WITH LIFE AND SHARED SURREALISM'S ENTHUSIASM FOR CHANCE ENCOUNTERS. HE PUT LAMANTIA INTO HIS NOVELS AS THE MAD GENIUS POET FRANCIS DEPAVIA OR DAVID DIANGELI.

RING RING RING RING RING

THE ONLY ONES FOR ME ARE THE MAD ONES, MAD TO LIVE, MAD TO TALK, DESIROUS OF EVERYTHING AT THE SAME TIME

WHO BURN BURN BURN LIKE FABULOUS ROMAN CANDLES EXPLODING

TI-JEAN, IT'S SOMEONE CALLED LAMANTIA

(Kerouac at home with his mother)

HEY, AMAZING CHANCE, I WAS JUST WRITING ABOUT YOU.

I'M WORKING ON A NEW BOOK, I'M GOING TO CALL IT *NEW HOBOES ON THE ROAD*...

...HMM.. YOU THINK IT SHOULD BE SHORTER.. *ON THE ROAD*...

PHILIP WAS IN MOROCCO MOST OF 1952, HANGING OUT WITH PAUL BOWLES, WHO WAS RECORDING ARAB AND BERBER FOLK, SACRED, AND POPULAR MUSIC.

IN 1953, PHILIP AND THE ARTIST GOLDIAN NESBIT JOINED THE PEYOTE RITES OF THE WASHO TRIBE IN CALIFORNIA'S SIERRA MADRE.

THE MAGIC OF THE IMAGINATION RETURNS TO LIFE, HERE IT IS A LIVING FORCE!

LAMANTIA INTERMITTENTLY USED PEYOTE AND OTHER DRUGS TO DISORDER HIS SENSES AND PROVOKE ENLIGHTENMENT.

IN THE 50'S PHILIP MET LEONORA CARRINGTON IN MEXICO. SHE WORKED ON PAINTINGS WHILE TALKING IN THREE LANGUAGES. LEONORA CREATED A WORLD OF MAGIC WHEREVER SHE WENT.

LEONORA, YOU ARE A SEER!

IT IS THE RIGHT EYE'S DUTY TO DIVE INSIDE THE TELESCOPE WHILE THE LEFT EYE INTERROGATES THE MICROSCOPE.

EXACTLY!

AT MIDNIGHT ON THE PYRAMID OF THE SUN, PHILIP HAD A TERRIFYING PREMONITORY VISION OF THE END OF HUMAN LIFE ON EARTH. HE READ HIS POEM ABOUT IT TO HIS FRIENDS ERNESTO CARDENAL AND HOMERO ARIDJIS.

¡¡OH POBRE HUMANIDAD!! EN ESTA PLANETA TU TIEMPO HABRA TERMINADO!

ALL THIS POETRY MUST GO! A PHOENIX WILL RISE FROM THE ASHES!

PHILIP CONTINUED TO HAVE BEATIFIC AND INFERNAL VISIONS. WHILE STAYING WITH THE CORA INDIANS IN NAYARIT, HE WAS BITTEN BY A SCORPION AND RECEIVED A POWERFUL MYSTICAL REVELATION. SOON AFTERWARD HE BURNED MOST OF HIS MANUSCRIPTS.

OCTOBER 7, 1955

PHILIP WAS PART OF THE FAMOUS SIX GALLERY READING.

HE ASTONISHED EVERYONE BY NOT READING HIS OWN POEMS BUT THOSE OF HIS FRIEND JOHN HOFFMAN, WHO HAD RECENTLY DIED IN MEXICO.

ONE OF PHILIP'S GOOD FRIENDS IN SAN FRANCISCO WAS BOB KAUFMAN.

HI, BOB, WHAT'S NEW?

HERE'S MY ABOMUNIST MANIFESTO, I HOPE YOU DIG IT!

LET'S SEE...

ABOMUNISTS VOTE AGAINST EVERYONE BY NOT VOTING FOR ANYONE...ABOMUNISTS READ NEWSPAPERS ONLY TO ASCERTAIN THEIR ABOMINUBILITY... LAUGHTER SOUNDS ORANGE AT NIGHT, BECAUSE REALITY IS REALIZATION WHILE IT EXISTS...

THIS IS COOL!

PHILIP CONSIDERED SABATO SIMON RODIA'S WATTS TOWERS ONE OF THE GREAT MARVELS OF THE HUMAN SPIRIT.

THERE ARE 17 TOWERS, THREE OF THEM OVER 99 FEET TALL TO BE EXACT. I BUILT THEM BY HAND.

IT TOOK ME 33 YEARS!

PHILIP WENT ON THE ROAD, WITH LONG STAYS IN FRANCE, ITALY, MOROCCO, AND SPAIN. HE MET HIS FUTURE WIFE, NANCY J. PETERS, IN ATHENS IN 1965.

VERY IMPORTANT. YOU MUST TELL ME EVERYTHING YOU KNOW ABOUT THE MOON.

WHILE WALKING DOWN THE STREET IN PARIS, PHILIP HAPPENED TO ENCOUNTER TED JOANS AND THE EGYPTIAN SURREALIST POET JOYCE MANSOUR.

ARE YOU GOING TO THE POETRY FESTIVAL IN LONDON?

NO! FOR ME THERE'S ONLY EGYPT! ESOTERIC GEOMETRY! THE SYMBOLIQUE! I MUST FIND THE KEY TO THE GREAT MYSTERY!

AH, TO BE POSSESSED BY A DEMON ONE MUST WANT TO BE POSSESSED.

POETRY WILL DISPEL DEMONS!

I'M RETURNING TO MY SURREALIST ROOTS LIKE AN ACT OF NATURE.

PHILIP WENT TO SPAIN, LIVED WITH NANCY IN MALAGA. HE BEGAN TO WRITE POETRY AGAIN AFTER A LONG SILENCE.

FERLINGHETTI PUBLISHED LAMANTIA'S SELECTED POEMS IN HIS POCKET POETS SERIES. THE COLLECTION ALSO INCLUDED POEMS FROM LAMANTIA'S EARLIER BOOKS *EROTIC POEMS, TOUCH OF THE MARVELOUS, EKSTASIS,* AND *DESTROYED WORKS.*

CITY LIGHTS BOOKS

BOOKS

HE WROTE TO PHILIP IN SPAIN:

...I'VE WANTED TO PUBLISH A BOOK OF YOURS FOR A LONG TIME.

PHILIP AND NANCY MADE TRIPS TO THE SOUTHWEST TO SEE HOPI AND OTHER NATIVE AMERICAN POETS.

GREEN CORN MAKES A WHITE BUTTERFLY INTO AN OBELISK TRAVELING AT NIGHT.

146

LAMANTIA AND NANCY PETERS CONTRIBUTED TO THE SURREALIST JOURNALS ARSENAL AND FREE SPIRITS. THEY ATTENDED THE WORLD SURREALIST EXHIBITION IN CHICAGO IN 1976.

Franklin & Penelope Rosemont

IN THE 1980'S, LAMANTIA HELPED ORGANIZE BENEFITS FOR PRESERVING TRADITIONAL HOPI AND NAVAJO LANDS.

THE KEY TO THE FUTURE LIES IN THE OLD WAYS.

SETTLING PERMANENTLY IN SAN FRANCISCO, LAMANTIA EMBRACED RADICAL ECOLOGY, PUBLISHED BLOOD OF THE AIR AND BECOMING VISIBLE, AND TAUGHT COURSES IN THE POETIC IMAGINATION AT SF STATE UNIVERSITY AND THE SF ART INSTITUTE.

WHAT'S THIS? THERE ARE OVER 5,000 BOOKS ON THIS RECOMMENDED READING LIST!

IT'S SAD HOW LITTLE THEY'VE BEEN EXPOSED TO!

RADIC

IN SPITE OF TWO DECADES OF DEBILITATING BIPOLAR ILLNESS, PHILIP CONTINUED TO HAVE PERIODS OF BRILLIANT LUCIDITY, WHEN HE GAVE MESMERIZING READINGS AND SPENT TIME WITH YOUNG, SURREALIST-ORIENTED POETS. CITY LIGHTS PUBLISHED HIS BED OF SPHINXES: NEW AND SELECTED POEMS IN 1997.

THE MARVELOUS TOUCHED HIM.

IT WAS HIS LIFE.

Story: Harvey Pekar

Art: Peter Kuper

It took Gary Snyder, one of the most important American poets of the 1950's, a fairly long time to even realize he was a poet.

He grew up in rural Washington and Oregon and soon developed an attachment to the land, doing a lot of skiing and mountaineering.

He also had a keen interest in Native American cultures.

He attended Reed College in Portland, supporting himself in the summer as a logger or working for the forest service. Early on he was into Buddhism and eventually took classes in Chinese and Japanese at U.C. Berkeley to learn about it directly.

In 1956 he moved to Japan and lived there for twelve years, studying Zen Buddhism and meditating.

Snyder had been interested in poetry as a young man and had written some himself. However, at Reed College he hung around with two fine poets, Philip Whalen and Lew Welch,

Early on he was influenced by D.H. Lawrence, and then Stevens, Yeats, and Eliot. When working in the northern part of Yosemite Park he was inspired to put even more effort into writing poems. His work had by then been influenced by Chinese writing.

and this heightened his involvement with it.

148

On October 7, 1955, Snyder was one of the poets who read with Ginsberg, who that night created a sensation with "Howl."

I'D LIKE TO READ "THE BERRY PIECE."

His first published works, *Riprap* and *Myths and Texts*, came out in 1959 and 1960. One commentator mentioned that in them "Snyder wants to be considered a poet of the ordinary man."

Don McLeod noted that "The poet-shaman (Snyder) draws his songs from the (Earth) Mother Goddess and through the magic power of image,

metaphor, MUSIC, and myth creates the artistic patterns that express the most deeply held knowledge and values of the community."

On his return to the USA Snyder continued his excellent work and won the 1975 Pulitzer Prize for poetry with his *Turtle Island*.

THE BEATS, INCLUDING **KEROUAC** and **CASSADY**, HAVE A WELL-EARNED REPUTATION AS MISOGYNISTS, YET DIANE di PRIMA (born AUGUST 6, 1934), MANAGED TO SURVIVE THAT AND BECOME ONE OF THE BEST-KNOWN **BEAT POETS** AND, INDEED, PERSONALITIES.

SHE WAS BORN IN NEW YORK, THE GRANDDAUGHTER OF ITALIAN IMMIGRANTS. HER GRANDFATHER **DOMENICO MALLOZZI** WAS AN ACTIVE ANARCHIST and A DIE-HARD FREE THINKER. HE DIED OF A BAD HEART WHEN di PRIMA WAS ONLY 11, BUT HIS INFLUENCE ON HER WAS PROFOUND and PROPHETIC.

AT HUNTER HIGH SCHOOL, SHE WAS AN OUTSTANDING STUDENT and EARNED A SCHOLARSHIP TO SWARTHMORE COLLEGE. AFTER TWO UNFULFILLING YEARS, SHE DECIDED TO QUIT, MOVED TO THE LOWER EAST SIDE, and, AT 18, PURSUED HER CAREER AS A WRITER and QUICKLY FOUND A COMMUNITY OF ARTISTS, DANCERS, and MUSICIANS.

DI PRIMA STARTED WRITING AT AGE 7 BUT HER FIRST BOOK, *This Kind of Bird Flies Backward*, WAS PUBLISHED IN 1958 BY LE ROI and HETTIE JONES'S TOTEM PRESS. LE ROI and DIANE CO-EDITED *The Floating Bear*, A LITERARY JOURNAL DEDICATED TO NEW IDEAS. THEY WERE ARRESTED FOR "OBSCENITY" FOR THE 9TH ISSUE. JONES DEFENDED THEIR IDEAS BEFORE A GRAND JURY and THE CASE WAS THROWN OUT.

SOCIETY WAS REDEFINING MORES and SEXUAL ACTIVITIES AND di PRIMA EMBRACED THE PHILOSOPHY "I AM HUMAN, THEREFORE NOTHING IS FOREIGN TO ME." SHE RAISED HER FIRST DAUGHTER, ALONE—BY DESIGN—and LATER HAD A SECOND DAUGHTER BY LE ROI JONES. HER LIFE JOURNEY HAS PRODUCED **FIVE CHILDREN.**

Di PRIMA ALSO CO-FOUNDED **THE NEW YORK POETS THEATRE,** WHICH COMBINED DANCE, POETRY, and EVERYTHING FROM "BURLESQUE TO BAUHAUS." IT LASTED FOUR SEASONS... ONE-ACT PLAYS and ART "HAPPENINGS." (LATER, di PRIMA BOUGHT AN OFFSET PRINTING PRESS and BECAME A PUBLISHER OF LIMITED EDITIONS—**POETS PRESS.**)

151

BEFORE FINALLY SETTLING IN SAN FRANCISO, di PRIMA WAS A **SEEKER**...LIVING AT A ZEN ASHRAM, BEING A PART OF MILLBROOK, TIM LEARY'S PSYCHEDELIC COMMUNITY. IN S.F., SHE WORKED WITH **THE DIGGERS**, A POLITICAL GRASSROOTS TROUPE...HER INFLUENCES AT THIS TIME WERE ALLEN GINSBERG and EZRA POUND. THIS WAS ALSO WHEN HER *Revolutionary Letters* WAS WIDELY PUBLISHED UNDERGROUND.

IN SAN FRANCISCO SHE BECAME DEEPLY INVOLVED WITH BUDDHISM AND LATER TAUGHT AT THE BUDDHIST NAROPA INSTITUTE IN BOULDER, COLORADO. IN 1983, AFTER 20 YEARS OF PRACTICING ZEN, di PRIMA BECAME A STUDENT OF CHÖGYAM TRUNGPA and LAMA THARCHIN.

PERHAPS HER FINEST WORK IS HER EPIC, *Loba* (1978), THE WOLF GODDESS EXPLAINED and VERBALLY SCULPTED AS di PRIMA ADDRESSESS THE MANIFESTATION OF FEMALE POWER IN A MYTHOLOGICAL CONTEXT.

IN 2001, di PRIMA FINISHED HER AUTOBIOGRAPHICAL MEMOIR, *Recollections Of My Life As a Woman*. THIS BOOK IS REALLY **PART ONE** OF HER LIFE. DiPRIMA'S EXPERTISE INCLUDES HEALING, TAROT, and MAGICAL PRACTICES. HER WORK SPANS **60 YEARS, 30 BOOKS**, AND **THOUSANDS OF POEMS**. SHE FACED EVERY CHALLENGE DIRECTLY and WITH COURAGE, EARNING HER PLACE ALONGSIDE THE MEN AS AN INTEGRAL PART OF **THE BEAT GENERATION**.

TEXT: PEKAR and FLEENER

ART: © M. FLEENER · 2007

Slim Brundage was a bohemian from the beginning. Nothing about his birth or upbringing could be considered mainstream. Born Myron Reed Brundage in Blackfoot, Utah, in 1903, he was named after "a renegade Methodist preacher who taught the Bible according to Karl Marx" (53). He was always proud of the fact that he was born in the lunatic asylum where his mother worked. For his part, his father put out a weekly newspaper all by himself when he was not "digging ditches" or doing other odd jobs "between revolutions," as Slim put it.

APOLOGIES TO WATTERSON, BREATHED, AND FOX

His childhood was difficult, but he was difficult back. His mom died when he was seven, leaving his father to raise three boys. At ten, Slim was placed in an orphanage, where he organized a strike against its strict rules and lousy food. (He got the other kids to refuse to say their prayers.) "The heads hollered that Pop should take me out before I wrecked the morale of the joint ... He did" (53).

All quotes from *From Bughouse Square to the Beat Generation: Selected Ravings of Slim Brundage, Founder and Janitor of the College of Complexes*, edited by Franklin Rosemont, Charles H. Kerr Press, Chicago, 1997

Praise God, from Whom all bless-ings flow; Praise Him, all crea-tures here be-low;
PRAISE BOSS WHEN MORNING WORKBELLS CHIME; PRAISE HIM FOR BITS OF O-VER-TIME!
Praise Him a-bove, ye heav'n-ly host; Praise Fa-ther, Son, and Ho-ly Ghost.
PRAISE HIM WHOSE WARS WE LOVE TO FIGHT; PRAISE HIM FAT LEECH & PA-RA-SITE!

At sixteen, Slim went hoboing and worked as a farmhand and fruit picker. He was frequently jailed for vagrancy and put on chain gangs. He joined an unusual labor union called the Industrial Workers of the World, or "Wobblies." They took everyone regardless of race, occupation, or employment status when other unions discriminated, focused only on particular crafts, and ignored the unemployed. Accordingly, the Wobblies organized migrant workers and got involved in hobo culture. They wrote scathing parodies of Salvation Army hymns that the sermon-weary poor and unemployed greatly appreciated.

In 1922, Slim landed in Chicago, a major railroad hub and the capital of hobo culture. At rowdy open forums such as the Bug Club, Bughouse Square, and the Dil Pickle Club, hoboes and other working folk built their own informal educational institutions to share stories and information. These meeting places attracted all kinds of agitators, artists, and musicians. The Dil Pickle, for example, was the main hangout for the Windy City's Dadaists, who were just as active as Paris's or Berlin's (23). Anybody could say anything in such places.

Slim, who was fascinated by all viewpoints and art forms, had come home to "hobohemia." There after, he had a hand in Chicago's counter culture for the next half century. He worked at the Dil Pickle in 1924 and managed another hobo college called the Knowledge Box in 1935. In between, he married Margaret Johnson, who, as "M. Brundage," painted many covers for *Weird Tales*, the magazine that introduced H. P. Lovecraft and Robert E. Howard.

After a few false starts, Slim opened his own place in 1951. He called it the College of Complexes and, true to his egalitarian ethos, he called himself the "Janitor" rather than the owner or manager. Billed as "The Playground for People Who Think" the college was also described as "a kind of modern-urban-nightclub version of Brook Farm" (11). Part bar, part debate club, it had wall-to-wall blackboards and operated like its predecessors. Everyone was welcome and every idea was entertained and made entertaining. Regulars were called "schizoids" and their rants "neuroses." This was probably in honor of Slim's birthplace, but "bug house" was hobo slang for asylum, so there was precedent.

As one regular recounted, "What he did was make it fun to think, fun to play with ideas, fun to speak up and to hell with the censors!" Slim said, "There are No Trespassing signs on the minds of men as well as on real estate," and as a former hobo he, of course, ignored them (24). The debate and group discussion topics published in the college's house organ, *The Curriculum*, gives an idea how lively things got: "Was Karl Marx a Schnook or a Good Guy?" "Will Sex Ever Displace Baseball as a National Pastime?" "Why Do All World War II Novels Stink?" and "Why the Next President Should Be Shot Into Space" (12).

Culturally, the College of Complexes was a universal venue. It attracted such diverse luminaries as Carl Sandburg, Duke Ellington, Studs Terkel, and Tony Bennett. As Franklin Rosemont, the editor of Slim's works, wrote, "A wide variety of music was played there: folk, jazz, blues, ethnic, classical, and tin-pan-alley. Big Bill Broonzy often played at the Wednesday evening Folk Nights; Ella Jenkins was a college 'regular' for years. Where else but the College could you listen to live music played on a Japanese samisen, Hungarian cymbaline, Scottish bagpipes and Russian balalaika – all in one night? Many evenings were given to the art of dance: African, Afro-Cuban, Latin American, modern, social jazz and even square" (13).

The place became Chicago's primary beatnik bistro. "From mid-1958 through the closing of the College in May 1961, Beat activities and polemics dominated *The Curriculum*. Beatnik Poetry Nights, Beatnik Party Nights, Beat plays (notably Jack Gelber's *The Connection*), harangues by Beats and anti-Beats and supporters of Beats were daily affairs" (32). In 1959, the college mocked the Miss America Pageant by holding its own "Miss Beatnik" contest. In 1960, syndicated columnist Dorothy Kilgallen wrote, "If you wish to see the so-called 'beat generation' *in action*, drop by the College of Complexes" (32).

The pageant was not the college's most outrageous spoof. In 1960, Brundage founded the Beatnik Party, which held a convention in New York City to nominate its anti-presidential and anti-vice-presidential candidates. Slim said the aim was "to lampoon the hell out of the powers that be" (33). "Don't get out the vote!" was one of its slogans, and its anarchist-inspired platform called for the immediate abolition of money, government, and work.

The college was getting attention. Brundage had opened a New York branch and almost pulled off launching another in San Francisco. But in 1961, the IRS closed the college down, claiming that it owed a vast sum in back taxes. This was odd because the agency had previously assured Slim that it was paid up. Was this punishment for providing a forum for dissidents or mocking the two-party system? The house that Slim built was closed, but its spirit lived on in the various teach-ins, be-ins, freedom schools, and free universities that followed.

Slim remained a public figure. "Once in a while you could catch the Janitor on radio or TV. I remember him one night on Kup's Show, shambling into the room in his rumpled gray outfit, slouching in a chair and scowling at everybody as he railed against one aspect and another of what used to be called 'the American Way of Life.' As is often the case with curmudgeons, people tended to find him loveable. In 1965 the daily news featured him as one of the sixty-two 'Best People' in Chicago" (38). Mirthful discontent was always his hallmark. College graffiti called him "the kind of guy who could sit on a barrel of scotch in a harem and complain." Slim described himself as both "a foreigner in his own country" and "the luckiest man alive" (45). He died in 1990.

BEATNIK CHICKS

BY JOYCE BRABNER

ART J SUMMER McCLINTON

1961 WAS "THE UPSIDE DOWN YEAR." TURN THOSE NUMBERS UPSIDE DOWN AND THEY STILL READ THE SAME.

TURN A CULTURE UPSIDE DOWN AND EVERYTHING IS DIFFERENT: SQUARES VS. HIPSTERS.

WE WERE KIDS. WE WERE INFORMED BY CHILDREN'S BOOKS, TV COMEDIES, AND MAD MAGAZINE.

BEFORE LOUISE FITZHUGH WROTE HER FAMOUS "HARRIET THE SPY" BOOKS, SHE ILLUSTRATED THE STORY OF SUZUKI BEANE.

SUZUKI BEANE WAS A LITTLE BEATNIK GIRL WHO RAN AWAY WITH A LITTLE SQUARE BOY FROM AN UPPER-CRUST FAMILY THAT DISAPPROVED OF THEIR FRIENDSHIP.

AS DID SUZUKI'S PARENTS, HUGH AND MARSHA.

HUGH WAS A BEATNIK AND MARSHA WAS "A BEATNIK CHICK."

BEATNIK CHICKS WORE PIXIE CUTS OR LONG HAIR WITH BLUNT-CUT BANGS.

THEY DRESSED IN BLACK CLOTHES WITH BLACK TIGHTS.

SNAP!

THEY WERE SOMETHING TO LAUGH AT.

MANY WERE TOO SERIOUS AND TOO SMART.

THOSE BEATNIK CHICKS USUALLY WORE GLASSES THAT MADE THEM EVEN MORE FUNNY-LOOKING.

THERE WAS SUPPOSED TO BE SOMETHING RIDICULOUS ABOUT SMART, SERIOUS WOMEN WITH GLASSES.

(THE AUTHOR) —1961—

THAT WORRIED ME.

↑ (THE AUTHOR PRESENT DAY)

THERE WAS ALSO SUPPOSED TO BE SOMETHING FUNNY ABOUT SEXY BEATNIK CHICKS. THEIR CLEAVAGE DIDN'T SPILL OUT OF THEIR CLOTHES LIKE JAYNE MANSFIELD. THEY DIDN'T WIGGLE WHEN THEY WALKED LIKE MARILYN MONROE. BUT IN 1961,

SEXY WOMEN WERE ALSO SOMEHOW RIDICULOUS.

THEIRS WAS ANOTHER KIND OF SEXY, BEATNIK CHICKS GYRATING IN BLACK CATSUITS

AS BONGOS THUMPED IN COFFEE-HOUSES.

OR SULLEN DECORATIVE OBJECTS DRAPED SILENTLY ON THE ARMS OF THEIR MORE VOLUBLE PARTNERS, WHO WERE BEATNIK ARTISTS OR BEATNIK POETS.

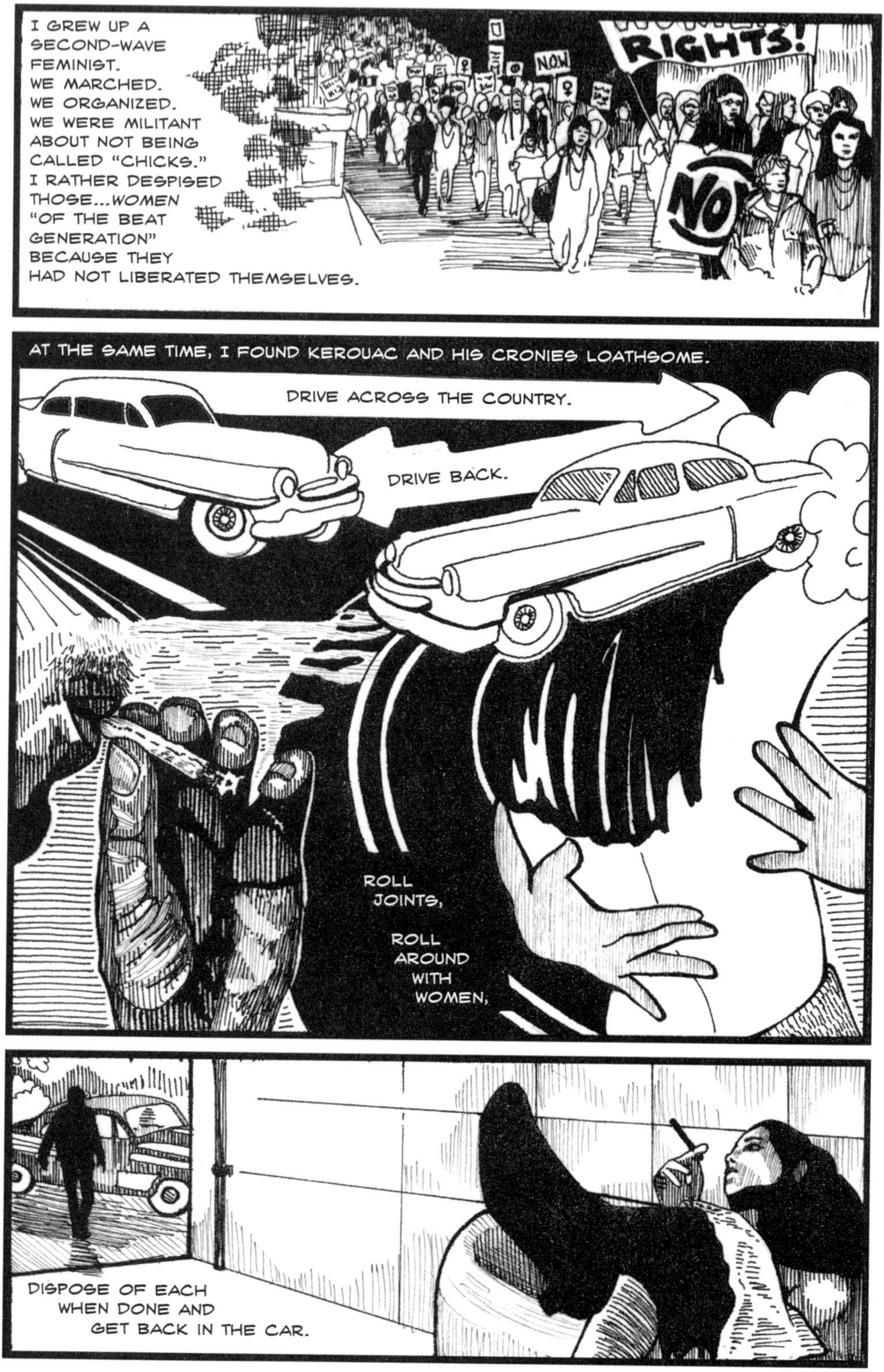

I GREW UP A SECOND-WAVE FEMINIST. WE MARCHED. WE ORGANIZED. WE WERE MILITANT ABOUT NOT BEING CALLED "CHICKS." I RATHER DESPISED THOSE...WOMEN "OF THE BEAT GENERATION" BECAUSE THEY HAD NOT LIBERATED THEMSELVES.

AT THE SAME TIME, I FOUND KEROUAC AND HIS CRONIES LOATHSOME.

DRIVE ACROSS THE COUNTRY.

DRIVE BACK.

ROLL JOINTS,

ROLL AROUND WITH WOMEN,

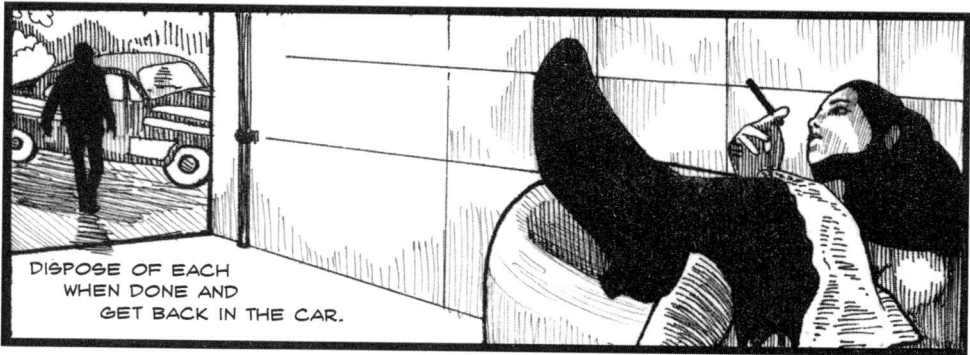

DISPOSE OF EACH WHEN DONE AND GET BACK IN THE CAR.

FASCINATE YOUR BUDDIES WITH EPIC TALES OF ROAD TRIPS TOLD IN RUN-TOGETHER SENTENCES LACED WITH AMPHETAMINE ARGOT, JAZZ JARGON.

 SELF-STYLED ODYSSEANS WHOSE ABANDONED CHILDREN GREW UP ANGRY. LIKE JAN KEROUAC.

JACK DENIED HE WAS HER FATHER.
A BLOOD TEST PROVED HE WAS.

HE "ALLOWED" HER HIS NAME, TO PUT ON THE COVERS OF ANY BOOKS SHE WROTE.

SHE DID.

I SUPPOSE I REMAINED INFORMED ABOUT BEAT WOMEN BY WHAT LITTLE I READ, TV COMEDIES AND MAD MAGAZINE, UNTIL THE RECENT EXPLOSION OF AUTOBIOGRAPHIES BY

JOYCE JOHNSON,

JOAN KEROUAC,

HETTIE JONES,

DIANE DIPRIMA,

CAROLYN CASSADY,

AND OTHERS.

THESE WOMEN WERE NOT ABSURD ORNAMENTS. AND THEY MADE MUCH POSSIBLE FOR WOMEN LIKE ME.

163

THEY WERE "Nobody's Wife"

LIKE JOAN KEROUAC.

OR COLLEGE GIRLS WHO DID NOT GRADUATE WITH THEIR "MRS. DEGREE."

MANY USED THEIR EDUCATION TO FIND JOBS IN PUBLISHING, WORKING BECAUSE THEY WANTED TO,

NOT BECAUSE THEY *HAD* TO, LIKE THEIR MOTHERS

WHO HAD "FILLED IN" FOR ABSENT SERVICEMEN DURING WORLD WAR II.

THEY DID NOT LIVE WITH THEIR PARENTS UNTIL MARRIED.

MANY TOOK APARTMENTS IN NEW YORK.

THEY SPENT LONG NIGHTS WRITING OR MAKING ART.

THEY HAD SEX BECAUSE THEY WANTED TO,

KNOWING SEX WAS DANGEROUS.

I MEAN, THERE'S JACK KEROUAC ALONE ON HIS MOUNTAINTOP HAVING VISIONS—

DETOXING FROM ALCOHOL AND DRUGS, ACTUALLY,

AND FILLING HIS NOTEBOOK WITH DREAMS AND WHAT LATER BECOMES A FAMOUS MANUSCRIPT.

WHILE AT THAT VERY SAME TIME HIS YET-TO-BE-MET LOVER JOYCE JOHNSON IS NEAR SHATTERED BY AN ILLEGAL ABORTION.

A LECHEROUS PLAYBOY HELPED HER FIND THE "DOC."

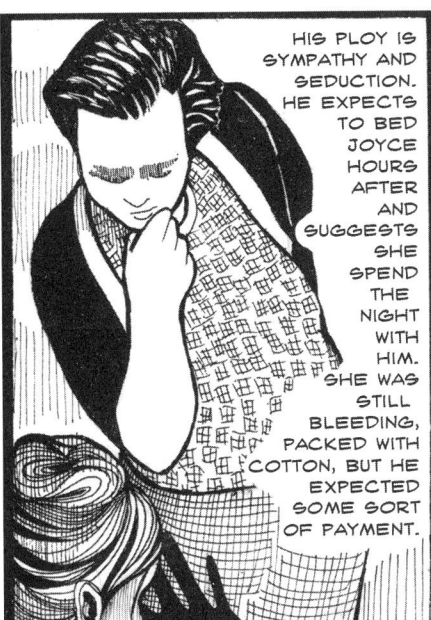

HIS PLOY IS SYMPATHY AND SEDUCTION. HE EXPECTS TO BED JOYCE HOURS AFTER AND SUGGESTS SHE SPEND THE NIGHT WITH HIM. SHE WAS STILL BLEEDING, PACKED WITH COTTON, BUT HE EXPECTED SOME SORT OF PAYMENT.

JOYCE KNOWS HE PULLS THIS SCAM ON ALL THE GIRLS HE "HELPS."

SHE RESISTS.

SHE WRITES ABOUT IT, ALTHOUGH NO ONE WILL READ THAT STORY UNTIL 1983.

JOYCE PUBLISHES ANOTHER KIND OF BOOK INSTEAD.

HER FRIEND ELISE COWAN IS DAZZLED BY A SEDUCTIVE YOUNG CHARMER NAMED ALLEN GINSBERG. LIKE HIM, SHE WRITES POETRY.

THEY MIRROR EACH OTHER AND POSE FOR A SERIES OF PHOTOGRAPHS "AS TWINS."

165

EAGER TO PLEASE HER PRESUMED SOUL MATE, SHE TYPES HIS LONG POEM "HOWL" AND DOES HIM OTHER FAVORS.

IT TAKES A WHILE FOR ELISE TO REALIZE THEY HAVE NO FUTURE TOGETHER. ALLEN IS QUEER.

IT TAKES A TOO-LONG WHILE FOR ELISE'S FRIENDS TO REALIZE HER SPIRALING DEPRESSION AND BIZARRE BEHAVIOR ARE MORE THAN JUST

CRAZY, MAN, CRAZY.

ELISE DRINKS, SHE DOES DRUGS, SHE WANDERS THE STREETS, AND DOES NOT SEEM TO CARE WHO IT IS SHE DRAGS BACK HOME TO HER BED.

SHE CROSSES THE COUNTRY, TRAVELING FROM GREENWICH VILLAGE TO SAN FRANCISCO.

HOW DIFFERENT WAS WHAT ELISE DID FROM WHAT WAS CELEBRATED IN BEAT BOY BOOKS ABOUT WANDERERS, ROAD TRIPS,

BEAUTIFUL BUMS, CARELESS INTOXICATION, AND EVEN MORE CARELESS SEX?

ELISE'S PARENTS DECIDE THEIR UNLADY-LIKE DAUGHTER MUST MOVE WITH THEM TO MIAMI.

IN RESPONSE ELISE HURLS HERSELF THROUGH A CLOSED GLASS WINDOW AND FALLS TO HER DEATH.

A CLOSED WINDOW.

WHAT FORCE, WHAT FURY MOVED HER?

ELISE WAS OUTSIDER TO THE OUTSIDERS.

A FEW OF HER POEMS ARE GATHERED AND SAVED FOR MUCH LATER PUBLICATION.

166

THE MIDDLE-CLASS, JEWISH HETTIE COHEN MARRIED THE MIDDLE-CLASS, AFRICAN-AMERICAN LEROI JONES.

HER FAMILY DENOUNCED HER.

THEY FOUND IT EASIER TO RAISE THEIR TWO DAUGHTERS IN THE CULTURAL MIX OF GREENWICH VILLAGE.

HETTIE'S FRIENDSHIP WITH JOYCE JOHNSON HELPED HER SURVIVE TOUGH TIMES OF NO MONEY AND EVEN LESS ENCOURAGEMENT.

HETTIE WROTE POEMS THAT SHE HID IN A DRAWER BECAUSE LEROI NEEDED HETTIE TO BE SECRETARY AND EDITOR OF A LITTLE MAGAZINE THAT PUBLISHED HIS WORK AND OTHER "REAL" WRITERS LIKE JACK KEROUAC AND GINSBERG.

LEROI NEEDED HETTIE TO UNDERSTAND HIS STORMY ROMANCE WITH THE POET DIANE DIPRIMA AND OTHER LIAISONS DURING THEIR MARRIAGE.

LEROI NEEDED HETTIE TO UNDERSTAND THAT SUPPORTING HIS FAMILY GOT IN THE WAY OF CREATIVE ENDEAVOR.

LEROI NEEDED HETTIE TO UNDERSTAND WHY HE WAS LEAVING HER AND CHANGING HIS NAME TO AMIRI BARAKA AFTER HIS HERO MALCOLM X WAS MURDERED.

LEROI NEEDED HETTIE TO UNDERSTAND THAT HE COULD NOT POSITION HIMSELF AS A BLACK NATIONALIST IF HE HAD A WHITE WIFE AND CARAMEL-COLORED CHILDREN.

NOR COULD HE PUBLISH HIS NEW ANTI-SEMITIC THEORIES WHILE MARRIED TO A JEWISH WOMAN.

HETTIE STRUGGLED WITH POVERTY, RAISED HER CHILDREN IN A BLACK COMMUNITY,

AND BECAME AN AWARD-WINNING POET AND TEACHER.

CLIK CLIK ☆ CLIK CLIK

SHE WROTE HER MEMOIRS BECAUSE:

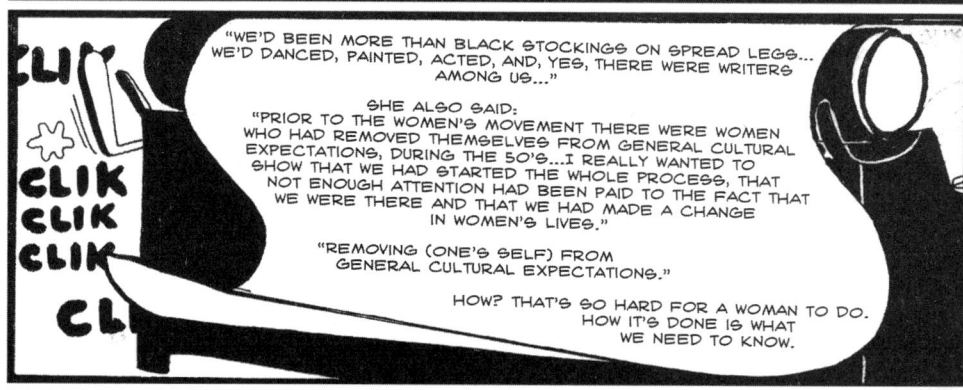

CLIK ☆ CLIK CLIK CLIK CLI

"WE'D BEEN MORE THAN BLACK STOCKINGS ON SPREAD LEGS... WE'D DANCED, PAINTED, ACTED, AND, YES, THERE WERE WRITERS AMONG US..."

SHE ALSO SAID:
"PRIOR TO THE WOMEN'S MOVEMENT THERE WERE WOMEN WHO HAD REMOVED THEMSELVES FROM GENERAL CULTURAL EXPECTATIONS, DURING THE 50's...I REALLY WANTED TO SHOW THAT WE HAD STARTED THE WHOLE PROCESS, THAT NOT ENOUGH ATTENTION HAD BEEN PAID TO THE FACT THAT WE WERE THERE AND THAT WE HAD MADE A CHANGE IN WOMEN'S LIVES."

"REMOVING (ONE'S SELF) FROM GENERAL CULTURAL EXPECTATIONS."

HOW? THAT'S SO HARD FOR A WOMAN TO DO. HOW IT'S DONE IS WHAT WE NEED TO KNOW.

I WAS NOT SATISFIED BY CAROLYN CASSADY'S MEMOIR.

YES, THAT GOLDEN CREATURE THREW DISCRETION TO THE WIND

AND PURSUED ESOTERIC OCCULT STUDIES AND THE ARTS.

SHE MARRIED NEAL CASSADY AND LOVED JACK KEROUAC,

WHO LOVED NEAL.

BUT ALL I REALLY REMEMBER

IS HOW CAROLYN STRUGGLED TO PROVIDE FOR THE CHILDREN SHE BORE WHILE NEAL ADVENTURED.

AND HOW NEAL ASKED HER TO BE PHOTOGRAPHED LOOKING SAD AND BEAUTIFULLY LONELY WHEN HE WAS DOING TIME FOR A DRUG BUST.

HE WANTED THE PICTURE TO SHOW THE PAROLE BOARD. IF IT AROUSED SYMPATHY, THEY MIGHT KICK HIM LOOSE EARLY.

I FIND SUCH IRONY TOO PAINFUL. I THINK THE GUY WAS A SOCIOPATH, DANGEROUS TO KNOW AND HURTFUL.

JOYCE JOHNSON BELIEVED THAT THE YOUNG WOMEN OF HER TIME ATTACHED THEMSELVES TO "DANGEROUS" MEN BECAUSE THEY, THEMSELVES, COULD NOT HAVE ADVENTURES.

THESE BAD BOYS OFFERED VICARIOUS THRILLS.

DIANE DI PRIMA (WHO WAS NO MERE HOMEWRECKER) INVENTED A DANGEROUS EROTIC ADVENTURE THAT SHE SOLD AS MEMOIRS OF A BEATNIK IN 1998.

OFFERING VICARIOUS THRILLS?

OR A WAY WOMEN'S SEXUAL IMAGININGS BECAME VISIBLE,

OUR OWN ODYSSEYS POSSIBLE.

DIANE WOULD MOVE ON, LEAVING BEHIND THE BEATNIKS OF NEW YORK BY ENTERING SAN FRANCISCO'S HIPPIE COUNTERCULTURE.

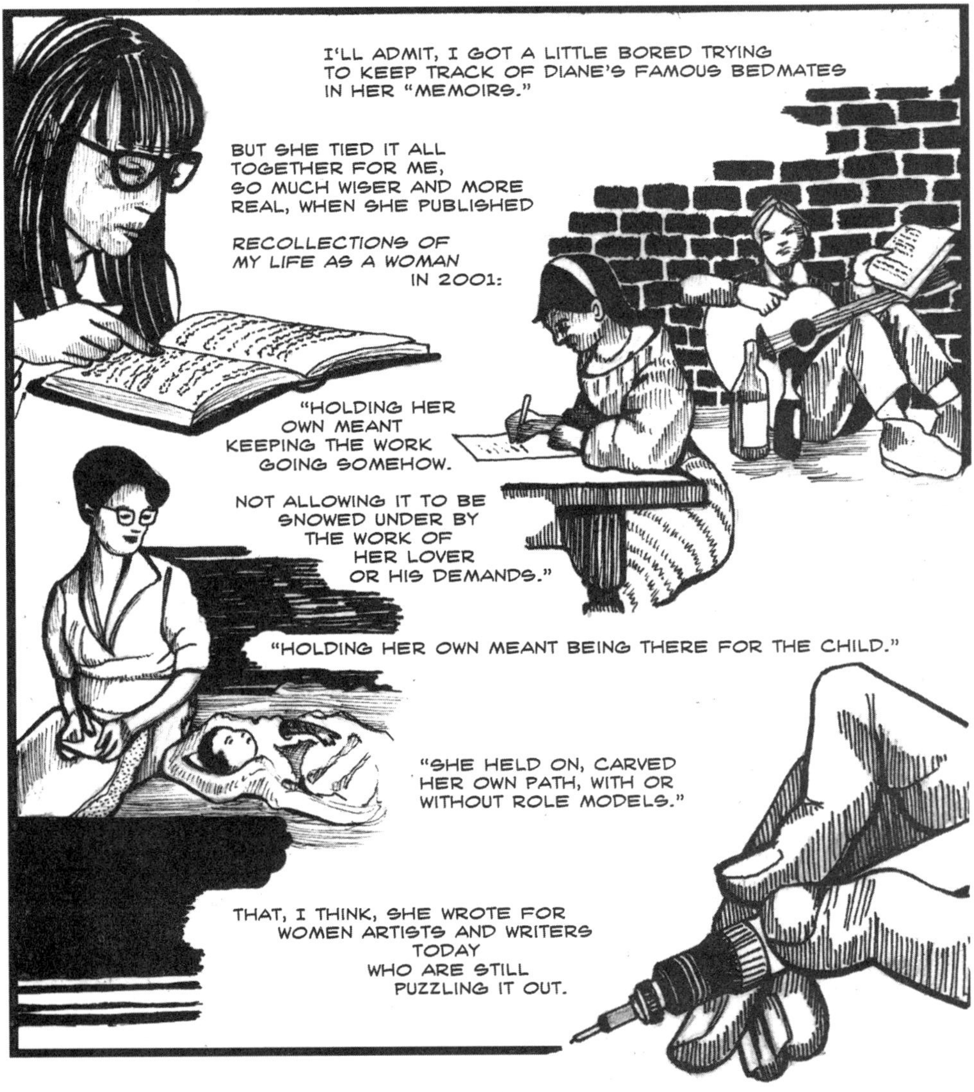

I'LL ADMIT, I GOT A LITTLE BORED TRYING TO KEEP TRACK OF DIANE'S FAMOUS BEDMATES IN HER "MEMOIRS."

BUT SHE TIED IT ALL TOGETHER FOR ME, SO MUCH WISER AND MORE REAL, WHEN SHE PUBLISHED

RECOLLECTIONS OF MY LIFE AS A WOMAN IN 2001:

"HOLDING HER OWN MEANT KEEPING THE WORK GOING SOMEHOW.

NOT ALLOWING IT TO BE SNOWED UNDER BY THE WORK OF HER LOVER OR HIS DEMANDS."

"HOLDING HER OWN MEANT BEING THERE FOR THE CHILD."

"SHE HELD ON, CARVED HER OWN PATH, WITH OR WITHOUT ROLE MODELS."

THAT, I THINK, SHE WROTE FOR WOMEN ARTISTS AND WRITERS TODAY WHO ARE STILL PUZZLING IT OUT.

170

Jay DeFeo: The Rose

STORY BY TRINA ROBBINS
ART BY ANNE TIMMONS

I SAW THE BEST MINDS OF MY GENERATION, STARVING, NAKED, HYSTERICAL...

GO! GO!

JAY DEFEO WAS ALREADY A WELL-KNOWN ARTIST AND PART OF THE SAN FRANCISCO BEAT MOVEMENT WHEN HER PAINTINGS WERE EXHIBITED AT THE SIX GALLERY ON OCTOBER 7, 1955, THE EVENING THAT ALAN GINSBERG FIRST INTRODUCED HIS NOW-FAMOUS POEM, "HOWL," TO THE WORLD.

MARCEL DUCHAMP IS ONE OF MY GREATEST GODS.

ABSTRACT EXPRESSIONISM IS IN THE AIR.

JAY NEVER THREW AWAY HER OLD CHRISTMAS TREES.

JAY AND HER ARTIST HUSBAND, WALLY HEDRICK, LIVED IN A FLAT ON FILLMORE STREET, WHERE BEAT POETS AND ARTISTS LIKE MICHAEL MCCLURE AND BRUCE CONNER HUNG OUT, READ THEIR POETRY, AND DISCUSSED THEIR ART.

171

SOMETIME IN 1958, JAY BEGAN WORK ON TWO PAINTINGS, *THE JEWEL* AND *THE ROSE*, ON 7 X 9 FOOT CANVASES.

AFTER SIX MONTHS, *THE JEWEL* WAS SET ASIDE, AND JAY DEVOTED HERSELF TO WORKING ON *THE ROSE*.

CERTAIN KINDS OF THINGS HAVE TO BE SAID IN A CERTAIN TIME.

FOR THE NEXT EIGHT YEARS, *THE ROSE* TOOK OVER HER LIFE, AS SHE PAINTED AND REPAINTED IT.

IT'S GOING THROUGH A WHOLE CYCLE OF ART HISTORY...

THE PRIMITIVE, THE ARCHAIC, THE CLASSIC, AND THEN ON TO THE BAROQUE...BUT STILL NOT THE FINAL VERSION.

SHE ENLARGED THE PAINTING BY GLUING IT ONTO AN EVEN LARGER CANVAS. NOW IT MEASURED 11 X 8 FEET.

I WANT TO CREATE A WORK THAT IS JUST SO PRECARIOUSLY BALANCED BETWEEN GOING THIS WAY OR THAT WAY THAT IT MAINTAINS ITSELF.

TO KEEP HERSELF GOING, JAY DRANK A QUART OF CHRISTIAN BROTHERS BRANDY A DAY AND SMOKED TWO TO THREE PACKS OF GAULOISES.

AT SOME POINT, SHE BEGAN ADDING METALLIC POWDERS INTO THE MIX FOR SPARKLE, AND INSERTED COPPER WIRE, BEADS, AND PEARLS.

JESUS, JAY, DID YOU JUST PUT A *BARRETTE* IN THERE?

PINE NEEDLES FROM JAY'S DEAD CHRISTMAS TREE COLLECTION FOUND THEIR WAY INTO THE PAINTING.

BY 1965, SHE HAD PAID A TOTAL OF $5,375.51 FOR PAINTING MATERIALS.

IN 1967, WALLY AND JAY LOST THE LEASE ON THEIR FILLMORE STREET APARTMENT.

OH MY GOD. HOW WILL WE *MOVE* IT?

173

TO GET THE PAINTING OUT, WORKERS HAD TO REMOVE THE ENTIRE WINDOW, ALONG WITH A TWO-FOOT SECTION OF WINDOWSILL.

UGH. MUST WEIGH A TON.*

* IT DID.

I REALLY WASN'T AWARE OF HOW FLAMBOYANT IT HAD BECOME...

... I WALKED INTO THE STUDIO ONE DAY AND THE WHOLE THING SEEMED TO HAVE GOTTEN COMPLETELY OUT OF HAND.

MOVERS

DESPITE ALL THOSE GAULOISES, IT WAS THE PAINTING THAT WAS THE DEATH OF HER. CONSTANTLY LICKING HER BRUSH TO GET A POINT, JAY INGESTED HUGE AMOUNTS OF LEAD FROM THE WHITE PAINT, AND DIED OF CANCER IN 1989.

THE ROSE WENT TO THE PASADENA MUSEUM OF ART, THEN TO THE SAN FRANCISCO ART INSTITUTE, WHERE IT STAYED FOR TWO DECADES, HIDDEN BEHIND A TEMPORARY WALL. DURING THIS TIME, EFFORTS WERE MADE TO SAVE THE PAINTING, FROM WHICH CHUNKS OF PAINT AND OTHER DEBRIS WERE FALLING.

TODAY IT RESIDES IN THE WHITNEY MUSEUM OF AMERICAN ART.

IRONICALLY, JAY'S FIRST TITLE FOR HER PAINTING HAD BEEN *DEATHROSE*.

MUCH INFORMATION IN THIS STORY COMES FROM *WOMEN OF THE BEAT GENERATION* BY BRENDA KNIGHT, 1996, AND QUOTES COME FROM A 1975 INTERVIEW WITH JAY BY PAUL KARLSTROM.

ART BEATS

AS **WRITERS** AND CELEBRATERS OF LIFE, **KEROUAC** AND THE BEATS **REBELLED** AGAINST THE STRICTURES OF CONFORMIST SOCIETY IN THE BLAND POST-WWII ERA. IN THE FACE OF **NUCLEAR ARMAGEDDON** THEY VALUED ARTISTIC AND PERSONAL FREEDOM OF EXPRESSION, BUT THEY CERTAINLY WEREN'T ALONE IN THIS. UNCONVENTIONAL **ABSTRACT EXPRESSIONIST ARTISTS** LIKE **JACKSON POLLOCK** (AKA "JACK THE DRIPPER") ALSO SWUNG TO A **JAZZ BEAT** ABLY SUPPLIED BY THE LIKES OF HIGH-FLYING SAXOPHONE GENIUS **CHARLIE "THE BIRD" PARKER** AND TRUMPETER **MILES DAVIS.**

STORY BY GARY DUMM AIDED BY PAUL BUHLE **ART** BY GARY DUMM

JACKSON POLLOCK

JACK KEROUAC

FURTHER, AS THE **SURREALISTS** BEFORE HIM HAD DONE, **POLLOCK'S "AUTOMISM** OR AUTOMATIC (ACTION) PAINTING" APPROACH ALLOWED HIM TO **CREATE** WITHOUT **OVERTHINKING...** AND IS A DIRECT PARALLEL TO **KEROUAC'S AUTOMATIC WRITING** TECHNIQUE (WHICH FLOWED LIKE A **JAZZ SOLO** IN THE SPONTANEOUS, UNFETTERED PROSE OF HIS NOVEL **ON THE ROAD,** TYPEWRITTEN ON A **CONTINUOUS** ROLL OF PAPER).

BUT **POLLOCK'S** ACTION PAINTING – USING THE DRIP OR POURING METHOD – MADE USE OF HIS **WHOLE** BODY, OR BEING, AND LIKE ONE OF "BIRD'S" MUSICAL IMPROVISATIONS WAS A **METAPHOR** FOR LIFE'S AND ART'S INFINITE **POSSIBILITIES.**

G. Dumm 2K7

SOME FEEL THAT THIS TECHNIQUE IS AKIN TO THE **NATIVE** AMERICAN ART OF **SAND PAINTING,** WHICH **CAN** PRODUCE AN ALTERED STATE OF **MIND/CONSCIOUSNESS** IN THE ARTIST WHILE CREATING.

KEROUAC WAS A FRIEND AND/OR ADMIRER OF THE ARTISTS POLLOCK, FRANZ KLINE, WILLEM DE KOONING, AND LARRY RIVERS (BORN YITZROK LOISA GROSSBERG). POLLOCK INADVERTENTLY BECAME A FAVORITE OF THE CULTURAL COLD WARRIORS, WHO, LIKE TIME MAGAZINE'S HENRY LUCE, TREATED ABSTRACT EXPRESSIONISM AS SO-CALLED "FREE ENTERPRISE" ART.

WILLEM DE KOONING

FRANZ KLINE

RIVERS, A "GRANDFATHER OF POP ART," BURST THE ABSTRACT EXPRESSIONIST BUBBLE WITH HIS SATIRICAL USE OF RECOGNIZABLE FIGURES, MOCKING CONSERVATIVES AND THEIR VALUES.

RIVERS

L.R. PAINTING WASHINGTON CROSSING THE DELAWARE.

AND RIVERS, WHO COLLABORATED WITH KEROUAC IN THE BEAT FILM PULL MY DAISY, WAS, LIKE GINSBERG, A RADICAL CRITIC OF U.S. POLICIES UNTIL THE END OF HIS LIFE.

ON THE ROAD OF LIFE SIMPLE ACTS CAN BE BOTH LIBERATING AND DANGEROUS, AND A CHANCE MEETING COULD BRING ANYTHING FROM ENLIGHTENMENT TO PREMATURE DEATH. IN THE EARLY FIFTIES AT THE SAN REMO OR CEDAR TAVERN IN NEW YORK CITY ONE MIGHT HAVE GLIMPSED POP CULTURE GIANTS AS THEY SHARED A DRINK, A SMOKE, AND A COUPLE OF LAUGHS OVER THE LATEST ISSUE OF SOME SUBVERSIVE PUBLICATION BEFORE HEADING OFF TO THEIR RESPECTIVE FATES.

FORTUNATELY THEY LEFT COLORFUL TRACES OF THEIR PASSING, MAKING US FAR RICHER FOR HAVING SHARED THEIR ARTISTIC EXPRESSIONS AND THEIR LITERARY VISIONS OF LIFE AND ART.

ON THE ROAD

THE END

JAZZ & POETRY text by HARVEY PEKAR illustrations by LANCE TOOKS

JAZZ AND POETRY WAS AT ITS MOST POPULAR IN THE LATE 50'S AND EARLY 60'S, BUT KENNETH REXROTH CLAIMS HE WAS EXPERIMENTING WITH IT IN 1927 IN CHICAGO.

HE WORKED WITH A BAND CALLED THE AUSTIN HIGH GANG, CONTAINING YOUNG MUSICIANS WHO WOULD LATER BECOME REVERED. HIS FAVORITE WAS DAVE TOUGH, AN OUTSTANDING DRUMMER WHO WAS KNOWN FOR HIS BOHEMIAN LIFESTYLE AND IMPRESSIVE INTELLECT. REXROTH CLAIMED TOUGH WAS AN ORIGINAL AND OUTSTANDING POET.

THERE WASN'T MUCH INTEREST IN JAZZ AND POETRY IN THE 1930'S BUT REXROTH KEPT AT IT, WORKING WITH CHARLES MINGUS DURING THE SECOND WORLD WAR.

THEN REXROTH WORKED AT THE CELLAR, A SAN FRANCISCO CLUB WHOSE OWNERS PLAYED IN THE HOUSE BAND.

the Cellar

SLOWLY JAZZ AND POETRY GAINED RECOGNITION. POET KENNETH PATCHEN EXPERIMENTED WITH IT.

ANOTHER NOTABLE EXPONENT OF
JAZZ AND POETRY WAS **BOB KAUFMAN**,
WHO HAD AN ORTHODOX GERMAN-JEWISH
FATHER AND A BLACK CATHOLIC MOTHER
FROM MARTINIQUE. KAUFMAN WAS A
NOTABLE SAN FRANCISCO PRESENCE IN
THE 1950's AND EARLY 60's.

THEN **STEVE ALLEN**, A JAZZ PIANIST,
RECORDED WITH **JACK KEROUAC**
AFTER HE'D BECOME FAMOUS.

LATER, KEROUAC RECORDED
WITH THE TENOR SAX STARS
AL COHN AND **ZOOT SIMS**.

THE RECORD WAS WELL RECEIVED.

SOON AFTER THAT, JAZZ AND POETRY WERE
"**IN**" WITH THE 60's BOHEMIANS, AND REMAINED
POPULAR FOR A SHORT TIME BEFORE FADING.

Like,
WOW!

Crazy,
Daddy...
Crazy!

?

SLAM

JAZZ AND POETRY REMAINS A VIABLE
ART FORM HOWEVER, AND COULD BE
CONSTRUCTIVELY REVIVED AT ANY TIME.

178

THE HARASSMENT OF d.a. levy

During the **1960's** it seemed like the local **COPS** and county **PROSECUTORS** in a number of **U.S.** cities had to have some **BEATNIK** or **HIPPIE** that they would **HASSLE** for using **SWEAR WORDS** in their poetry or smoking **MARIJUANA**. In Cleveland, Ohio, the **TARGET** was a young, quiet, and diminutive guy named d.a. (DARYLL ALLEN) levy.

STORY BY HARVEY PEKAR
PAGES 1 THRU 4
AND PAUL BUHLE
PAGE 5
ART BY
GARY DUMM

HE GRADUATED WITH A GOOD **ACADEMIC** RECORD FROM **JAMES FORD RHODES** HIGH SCHOOL AND JOINED THE **U.S. NAVY**, FROM WHICH HE WAS **DISCHARGED** FOR HAVING **MANIC-DEPRESSIVE** QUALITIES.

HE CAME BACK TO **CLEVELAND** **DETERMINED** TO BE A **POET**, AND HE DEVELOPED **RAPIDLY** AS ONE. HIS WORK WAS NOT ONLY **PRINTED** IN BOOKLET AND PAMPHLET FORM AROUND THE **CITY**, BUT PUBLISHED IN **UNDERGROUND** PAPERS ACROSS THE **COUNTRY**.

THE **COPS** AND **PROSECUTORS** IN THE CLEVELAND AREA SOON FOUND OUT ABOUT **LEVY** AND ACCUSED HIM OF BEING A **THREAT** TO LOCAL **YOUTH**...

...BECAUSE HE USED **SWEAR WORDS** IN HIS WRITING AND **ADVOCATED** THE LEGALIZATION OF **MARIJUANA**.

ALLEN GINSBERG AND THE **FUGS** FLEW IN FROM **NEW YORK** TO RAISE **MONEY** FOR **LEVY'S** DEFENSE.

180

LEVY'S POEMS WERE JUDGED **OBSCENE** IN A LOCAL **COURT**, AND HE WAS **SENTENCED** TO **SIX** MONTHS IN **JAIL** AND A **$100** FINE. THE CHARGES WERE **DROPPED** WHEN AN ASSISTANT COUNTY PROSECUTOR **NOTED** THAT RECENT SUPREME COURT **RULINGS** IN **OBSCENITY** CASES FAVORED THE **DEFENSE**.

BUT **LEVY** STILL FACED THE **PROBLEM** OF **SUPPORTING** HIMSELF. HE HAD LEARNED THAT VIRTUALLY NO **U.S. POETS** MADE A **LIVING** FROM INCOME FOR THEIR WORK.

AN **ACQUAINTANCE** OF MINE WHO WAS A FAN OF **LEVY'S** ANTIWAR **POEMS** RECALLS MEETING **LEVY** IN **MADISON, WISCONSIN**. HE NOTED THAT **LEVY** SEEMED **DEPRESSED**, PARTLY BECAUSE HE WAS SO **POOR**. HE GAVE **LEVY** A JOB TO DO AND **FIFTY** DOLLARS ON ITS **COMPLETION**, WHICH **LEVY** SPENT ON A **BUS TICKET** BACK TO **CLEVELAND**.

WHEN HE **RETURNED** HIS FRIENDS SAID THAT HE WAS DOING **"STRANGE STUFF"** SUCH AS **BURNING** ALL OF HIS **POETRY**. AFTER HAVING AN **ARGUMENT** WITH AND KICKING HER OUT OF THEIR **APARTMENT**, HIS **GIRLFRIEND** SAID THAT HE WAS **SITTING** AROUND WITH A **RIFLE**.

HOW **SYMBOLIC** WOULD IT BE IF I **BLEW** MY **BRAINS** OUT?

HE DID JUST **THAT, KILLING** HIMSELF IN LATE **NOVEMBER 1968**.

IN **PRAISE** OF d.a. levy AND THE WAYS IN WHICH HE BROUGHT POETRY TO A **CLEVELAND** WHOSE **LEADING** CITIZENS DID NOT UNDERSTAND HIM OR EVEN **WANT** HIM. FELLOW **POETS** SAW HIM **CLEARLY:**

DOUG BLAZEK

HERE IS A POET WHO USED **EVERYTHING** THAT HE LAID HANDS ON TO **HELP** FURTHER **CREATIVITY,** POETRY, POETS, AND TO HELP MAKE A **BETTER** WORLD.

IN A VERY **PURE** SENSE **LEVY** WAS A **TRUE REVOLUTIONARY.**

WE GET A **FEW** OF THESE PEOPLE PER **CENTURY.**

I FEEL **BROTHER** TO **LEVY** NOT **ONLY** AS POET, BUT AS FELLOW WORKER IN THE **BUDDHA**–FIELDS.

GARY SNYDER

BUT PERHAPS HE WAS SEEN, **MOST** REMARKABLY, AS A **TRANSITION** FROM THE **BEAT GENERATION** TO THE **HIPPIES.** THE YOUNG PEOPLE WHO **LISTENED** TO HIS MESSAGES AND TOOK THEM TO **HEART** WERE TOO YOUNG TO HAVE **KNOWN** THE **BEATS. LEVY** GAVE THEM A SERIOUS, IMPORTANT POETRY OF **POLITICAL** AND **SPIRITUAL** RESISTANCE THAT WAS IN THEIR **OWN** VEIN.

THE END

THERE IS PLENTY TO OBSERVE AND WRITE ABOUT, SEEN IN POEMS LIKE "GREENWICH VILLAGE 1958" AND "NOTES TOWARDS A THEORY OF BOHEMIANISM."

INTERRACIAL COUPLE HAND IN HAND ON MACDOUGAL STREET, THE LOVERS TOO HAPPY TO NOTICE THE EVIL STARES...

CHRISTMAS EVE ON HORATIO STREET, A BEAUTIFUL NAKED LESBIAN STORMS OFF DRUNK INTO THE NIGHT...

NO! NO! I WILL NOT COME BACK!!

CAN Y'HELP ME OUT WITH FARE TO HOBOKEN?

I GAVE HIM "FARE TO HOBOKEN" 20 MINUTES AGO AND HE DOESN'T EVEN REMEMBER BUMMING ME WITH THAT SAME LINE!

PLEASE DO NOT GIVE TO BEGGARS THANK YOU—MANAGE-MENT

STILL, THAT SHOPKEEPER'S SIGN IS WHAT DISGUSTS ME THE MOST.

AFTER ALL, ALL MERCHANTS ARE BEGGARS, SOME ARE SMALL SHOPKEEPERS, OTHERS ARE GIANT BEGGARS LIKE MACY'S.

AND GIANT DESTROYERS LIKE BOEING BOMBERS, DOW CHEMICAL, HALLIBURTON... THEY DESTROY AND REBUILD, MAKING MONEY ON BOTH ENDS.

IN 1958 TULI AND HIS GIRLFRIEND SYLVIA TOPP PUBLISH THE FIRST ISSUE OF "BIRTH."

IF SELF-PUBLISHING WAS GOOD ENOUGH FOR WHITMAN, IT'S GOOD ENOUGH FOR ME.

"BIRTH" INCLUDES WORK BY RAY JOHNSON, LEROI JONES, DIANE DI PRIMA, AND MANY OTHER BEAT CONTRIBUTORS OF ART AND POETRY. A SECOND AND THIRD ISSUE FOLLOW IN 1959 AND 1960.

185

TULI STARTS READING POETRY AT A PLACE ON 2ND AVENUE, DOWN SOME STEPS, CALLED THE METRO (OR CAFE LE METRO).

IT'S A BOOKIE PLACE, BUT TO COVER IT UP THE OWNERS STARTED HAVING READINGS.

EVERY-ONE READS HERE, FROM COMPLETE UNKNOWNS TO GINSBERG AND BURROUGHS...

AND THEY SELL FURNITURE HERE TOO!

$5⁰⁰

TULI MOVES TO 381 E. 10TH ST., BETWEEN B AND C, AND CONTINUES TO WRITE. IN 1961 HE PUBLISHES THE FIRST OF HIS SERIES OF "1,001" BOOKS, "1,001 WAYS TO LIVE WITHOUT WORKING."

51 - INVENT GUNPOWDER
52 - PRINT THE GUTENBERG BIBLE
53 - PRINT MONEY
54 - STEAL MONEY
55 - HAVE MONEY
56 - GET ALONG WITHOUT MONEY
57 - EAT SHIT (ETC., ETC.)

GREENWICH EGG MARKET

FROM 1961 TO '62, AT THE INDEPENDENT CHARLES THEATER ON AVE. B AND E. 12TH ST, JONAS MEKAS HOLDS WEEKEND MIDNIGHT AVANT-GARDE MOVIE SHOWS. IN FRONT OF ONE OF THESE, AN HISTORIC CONSULT TAKES PLACE...

HEY, YOU PUBLISHED "BIRTH" AND "BEATNIKS; OR THE WAR AGAINST THE BEATS," RIGHT? GOOD TO MEET YOU! MY NAME'S ED SANDERS.

YOU'RE THAT 22-YEAR-OLD FROM KANSAS CITY WHO WROTE "POEM FROM JAIL" AFTER BEING ARRESTED SWIM-MING TO STOP A NUCLEAR SUBMARINE!

CHARLES TH
MEKAS
GUNS OF THE TREES
THE FLOWER THIEF
TAYLOR MEAD
BIRTH
1,001 WAYS TO LIVE WITHOUT WORKING

(SELLING HIS WARES ON THE STREET)

WITH SHARED RADICAL AND POETIC INTERESTS, ED AND TULI BE-COME FRIENDS. ED BECOMES NOTORIOUS AS THE PUBLISHER OF "FUCK YOU/A MAGAZINE OF THE ARTS," TO WHICH TULI CONTRIBUTES.

A LITTLE WHILE LATER...

ED, THERE'S AN EMPTY KOSHER BUTCHER SHOP NEXT DOOR HERE—WEREN'T YOU LOOKING FOR A SPACE TO OPEN A BOOKSTORE NOW THAT YOU'VE GRADUATED NYU?

EGG MARKET
381
383
STREET TWO
BUTCHER
CLOSED

ED OPENS THE PEACE EYE BOOKSTORE AT 383 E. 10TH ST. IN 1964.

CHECK IT OUT, I GOT AN ORDER FOR "FUCK YOU" FROM A PRIEST!

YOU SELLIN' DRUGS IN THESE BAGGIES?

PEACE EYE BOOKSTORE

NO MAN, THAT'S MY NEW PRODUCT LINE, "PUBIC HAIRS OF THE POETS"!

IN ADDITION TO THE METRO IS A PLACE CALLED THE DOM, IN THE POLISH NATIONAL HOME ON ST. MARK'S PLACE—IT LATER HOUSES THE ELECTRIC CIRCUS.

THE DOM

PEOPLE ARE COMING TO THE VILLAGE FOR POETRY, PLAYS, THE SCENE IS GROWING. MORE PEOPLE ARE REACTING AGAINST THE VIETNAM WAR, AND AGAINST MAINSTREAM SOCIETY IN GENERAL.

ON A JUKE BOX THERE, ED AND TULI HEAR THE EARLY BEATLES—

LOVE, LOVE ME DO... YOU KNOW I LOVE YOU...

POP MUSIC IS ALL BOURGEOIS COURTSHIP CRAP—

WE CAN DO JUST AS GOOD—LET'S START OUR OWN BAND!

YEAH!

I DON'T THINK WE CAN GET AWAY WITH CALLING OURSELVES "THE FUCKS"...

IN "THE NAKED AND THE DEAD," NORMAN MAILER HAD TO SUBSTITUTE THE WORD "FUG" EVERY TIME HE HAS A SOLDIER SAY "FUCK"—LET'S BE "THE FUGS"!

THOUGH I HATE TO TELL YA, I AIN'T A MUSICIAN—THE ONLY THING I CAN PLAY IS THE RADIO.

THIS IS KEN WEAVER, AN AIR FORCE INTELLIGENCE VETERAN FROM EAST TEXAS—HE PLAYS CONGA DRUMS.

WHAT'S THAT FRAMED ON YOUR WALL, A DIPLOMA?

NAH, THAT'S MY DISHONORABLE DISCHARGE FOR SMOKIN' TOO MUCH DOPE!

SO WHADDA WE GONNA WRITE SONGS ABOUT? DOPE? FUCKING? LIFE ON AVENUE B?

YEAH, EVERYTHING! ED AND I HAVE WRITTEN LIKE 20 ALREADY. I WROTE A NEW ONE TODAY ABOUT NEEDING TO TAKE A SHIT ON THE SUBWAY...

AND THERE'S A LOT OF GREAT POETRY WE CAN SING—GINSBERG, BLAKE, SWINBURNE...

I'M GOING TO SING THE TEN COMMANDMENTS, TOGETHER WITH THE TEN AMENDMENTS.

AT AGE 41, TULI CO-FOUNDS THE MOST OUTRAGEOUS ROCK BAND OF ALL TIME - THE FUGS! FOR TULI, ED AND KEN THE SONGS COME FAST AND FURIOUS - POETIC, POIGNANT, OBSCENE, HILARIOUS, TABOO, FEARLESS, ANARCHISTIC - NO BOUNDARIES!
WHO CAN KILL A GENERAL IN HIS BED? OVERTHROW DICTATORS IF THEY'RE RED? C.I.A. MAN! FUCKIN'-A, MAN! C.I.A., MAN!
BOMPA BUMP BOMP
GROOVY CHICKS! UNDER 16! 12-INCH DICKS! I NEED APOMORPHINE! HALLUCINATION HORRORS... THAT'S WHAT I'VE GOT... HALLUCINATION HORRORS...
I GOBBLED UP A CUBE OF LSD... I WAITED 30 MINUTES FOR MY BODY TO SING... I WAITED AND I WAITED BUT I COULDN'T FEEL A THING!!
SHAKE SHAKE
BUMPADA BAMP
BECAUSE I COULDN'T GET HIIIGH... I DON'T KNOW WHY...
SLUM GODDESS FROM THE LOWER EAST SIIIDE... SLUM GODDESS, GONNA MAKE HER MY BRIIIDE... THERE'S NOT A CHICK IN THE WORLD AS HALF AS HIP AS SHE... MY SWINGIN' LITTLE GODDESS FROM AVENUE D...
IN THE KEY OF METAPHYSICAL DISTRESS - THE SWINBURNE STOMP!
KNOCK KNOCK
HOLD ON, I'LL GET THE DOOR...
THIS IS MY NEIGHBOR STEVE - HE PLAYS IN THAT WEIRD DRUG-FREAK FOLK DUO THE HOLY MODAL ROUNDERS.
WE HEARD YOU HAD A ROCK BAND WRITIN' DIRTY SONGS, MAN! WE WANNA JOIN!
WE'VE EVEN GOT SOME WE WROTE FOR YA... "BOOBS A LOT"... "NEW AMPHETAMINE SHRIEK"...
AND THEY EVEN PLAY INSTRUMENTS!
STEVE WEBER
PETER STAMPFEL
FEBRUARY 1965: PARTIALLY DUE TO ED'S UNDERGROUND REPUTATION, THE FUGS' DEBUT PERFORMANCE AT THE PEACE EYE BOOKSTORE IS A HIGHLY ANTICIPATED LOCAL EVENT! THE HOLY MODAL ROUNDERS PLAY TOO. KEN DRUMS ON AN EMPTY FRUIT CRATE, HIS CONGA DRUM HAVING RECENTLY BEEN STOLEN.
WE'RE THE FUUUGS... WE HATE WAR... WE LOVE SEX...
HEY, A REPORTER FROM TIME MAGAZINE IS HERE! HEH, BURROUGHS IS WALKING OUT ON US THOUGH...
TONIGHT THE FUGS
I MAKE "FIELD RECORDINGS" AND I WANNA GET YOU GUYS RECORDED.
THIS IS HARRY SMITH, HE MAKES THOSE CRAZY PSYCHEDELIC ANIMATED MOVIES...
I CAN GET YOU ON SMITHSONIAN FOLKWAYS RECORDS, I KNOW MOE ASCH FROM WHEN I COMPILED THE ANTHOLOGY OF AMERICAN FOLK MUSIC FOR THEM IN 1952...
COOL!

THE FUGS PLAY MORE SHOWS AROUND THE NEIGHBORHOOD AND WORD ABOUT THEM SPREADS. APRIL 1965: TULI, ED, KEN, STEVE, AND PETER, HAVE 3 HOURS IN A RECORDING STUDIO TO LAY DOWN AS MANY FUGS SONGS AS THEY CAN, LIVE TO TAPE.

WHY THE HECK IS A RESPECTABLE FOLK LABEL RECORDING **OUR** STUFF?

HARRY TOLD THEM WE'RE A "JUG BAND"... THO I THINK I KNOW WHERE THE "JUG" IS...

GLUG GLUG GLUG

MORE SOLD-OUT SHOWS FOLLOW—DOZENS, THEN HUNDREDS, AT PLACES LIKE THE PLAYER'S THEATER ON MACDOUGAL, IZZY YOUNG'S FOLKLORE CENTER, AND DIANE DI PRIMA'S AMERICAN THEATER FOR POETRY ON E. 4TH ST. POETS LIKE TED BERRIGAN CONTRIBUTE SONGS TO THEIR REPERTOIRE, PEOPLE LIKE ANDY WARHOL AND TENNESSEE WILLIAMS ATTEND THEIR SHOWS... THE FUGS ARE A COUNTERCULTURE SENSATION!

NOTHING LOTS AND LOTS OF NOTHING

IN JUNE '65 HARRY SMITH OVERSEES A SECOND 3-HOUR FUGS SESSION, THIS TIME WITHOUT PETER'S FIDDLE BUT ADDING ELECTRIC BASS AND GUITAR PLAYERS JOHN ANDERSON AND VINNY LEARY.

MR. SMITH, ONCE AGAIN I DON'T KNOW WHAT KIND OF SOUND YOU EXPECT ME TO GET WITH JUST THOSE MICS...

KILLERS & GOUGERS BUTCHERS & FREAKS DOPE-DEMONS & CREEPS THE QUEEN OF NAPALM PULLS OFF HER SKIN

BURP... *HIC...*

JUST KEEP THE FUCKIN' REEL ROLLING

SMASH!!!

YAAA

ED COMPILES WHAT HE THINKS ARE THE BEST SONGS FROM BOTH SESSIONS TO MAKE THE FUGS' FIRST ALBUM: "THE VILLAGE FUGS SING BALLADS OF CONTEMPORARY PROTEST, POINT OF VIEWS AND GENERAL DISSATISFACTION."

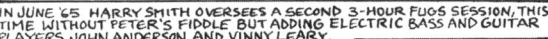

IN JULY

KILL FOR PEACE

being Yeah10

TULI SELF-PUBLISHES "KILL FOR PEACE," AN ILLUSTRATED CHRONICLE OF THE STUPIDITY OF WAR.

OCTOBER 1965: AS PART OF AN ANTI-VIETNAM WAR PROTEST, THE FUGS DO A BRIEF U.S. TOUR. THEIR VW TAKES THEM TO SAN FRANCISCO, WHERE THE FUGS WITNESS AND FAN THE EARLY SPARKS OF THE WEST COAST FLOWER POWER EXPLOSION.

WHEN THEY RETURN TO NEW YORK, THE ALBUM HAS ALREADY BEEN RELEASED, AND IT'S A SUCCESS. EVEN THE BEATLES IN ENGLAND ARE FANS!

PAUL, I RATHER WISH YOU WOULDN'T MAKE ME PLAY THIS AWFUL RECORD IN MY CLUB—

PLAY IT AGAIN, MAN! THESE GUYS FROM NEW YORK ARE **REALLY** FAR OUT!!

CARPE DIEM CARPE DIEM

FOR A WHILE PAUL McCARTNEY SIGNS HIS NAME AS "TULI KUPFERBERG" TO CONFUSE AUTOGRAPH-SEEKERS.

189

1967: THE CONSCIOUSNESS THAT STARTED IN A FEW MINDS AS THE "BEAT" SCENE IS EXPLODING INTO A NATIONWIDE 60'S COUNTERCULTURE, AND ED SANDERS IS FEATURED ON THE COVER OF **LIFE** MAGAZINE (FEB.17). A SECOND U.S. TOUR LANDS THE FUGS IN SAN FRANCISCO RIGHT IN THE "SUMMER OF LOVE."

OUR FUNKY VW BUS HAS BEEN BREAKING DOWN ALL TRIP LONG BUT IT WAS WORTH IT!

THIS IS LIKE PARADISE!

LOVE-IN

(AMUSING EPHEMERA, EXCERPTED FROM THE ALBUM ART OF THE 1967 LP "ELECTRIC COMIC BOOK" BY THE BAND THE BLUES MAGOOS--)

NO, IT COULDN'T BE

R. SCALA ORGANIST

I'LL JUST STAND HERE, HOLDING MY HANDS NICE... GIVE 'EM A CHANCE TO RECOGNIZE ME...

BUT LOOK AT THOSE GROSS SHOES

AND THOSE PSYCHEDELIC SUNGLASSES...

NOW I'LL LOWER MY SUNGLASSES TO HELP THEM A BIT...

THINK...

YES! OBVIOUSLY IT MUST BE...

TULI KUPFERBURG!

OH, RECOGNITIO

BOB WE BELIEVE THIS...

TULI PUBLISHES "1,001 WAYS TO BEAT THE DRAFT."

863 - TATTOO **WELCOME MEMBERS OF ALLIED FORCES** IN A CIRCLE AROUND YOUR ASSHOLE
864 - COME IN EATING A PIG'S HEAD
865 - COME IN EATING A DOG'S HEAD (ETC ETC)

1001 Ways to Beat the Draft

Grove Press

by Tuli Kupferberg & Robert Bashlow

(IMMEDIATELY AN UNDERGROUND CLASSIC, ITS MANY FANS INCLUDE FUTURE "SIMPSONS" CREATOR MATT GROENING.)

THE FUGS ARE "THE USO OF THE POLITICAL MOVEMENT," PLAYING PROTESTS AND BENEFITS, GOING TO DC FOR ALL THE DEMONSTRATIONS...

THE WAR IS KILLING EVERYBODY ON ALL SIDES - IF YOU'RE NOT INVOLVED IN ANTIWAR POLITICS YOU'RE AN IDIOT.

FUGS FOR PEACE

OCTOBER 21, 1967: THE FUGS AND CO. RALLY IN DC TO MENTALLY LEVITATE THE PENTAGON, EVEN RENTING A FLATBED TRUCK AND MEGAPHONES (FOR MORE ABOUT THIS DAY'S HAPPENINGS SEE NORMAN MAILER'S BOOK "THE ARMIES OF THE NIGHT").

ED LEADS A CROWD IN A "RITE OF EXORCISM"

JOIN THE Y.I.P.'S

FUCK THE WAR

...IN THE NAME OF DIONYSUS, ZAGREUS, JESUS, YAHWEH, THE UNNAMABLE, THE QUINTESSENT FINALITY OF THE ZOROASTRIAN FIRE... IN THE NAME OF THE TYRONE POWER POUND CAKE SOCIETY IN THE SKY... WE CALL UPON THE SPIRIT TO RAISE THE PENTAGON FROM ITS DESTINY AND PRESERVE IT...

OUT DEMONS OUT!! OUT DEMONS OUT!!

MP-56

A RECORDING OF THIS EVENT ("EXORCIZING THE EVIL SPIRITS FROM THE PENTAGON") IS RELEASED ON THE FUGS LP "TENDERNESS JUNCTION," THEIR FIRST FOR A MAJOR LABEL, REPRISE.

191

1968: THE YEAR THAT BOTH MARTIN LUTHER KING, JR., AND ROBERT KENNEDY ARE ASSASSINATED. IN ADDITION TO U.S. TOURS THE FUGS TOUR EUROPE TWICE AND RELEASE TWO ALBUMS. IN AUGUST ED AND TULI GO TO JOIN THE VOLATILE RALLIES AT THE DEMOCRATIC NATIONAL CONVENTION IN CHICAGO.

THE REST OF THE FUGS WERE TOO AFRAID TO COME...

I'M PRETTY FUCKING AFRAID TOO!

...I GIVE YOU A TRUE TESTIMONIAL...THE MC5!!

STUDENTS FOR A DEMOCRATIC SOCIETY SDS

National Mobilization to end the war in Vietnam

PEGASUS FOR PRESIDENT

YIPPIE!

THE WHOLE WORLD IS WATCHING!! THE WHOLE WORLD IS WATCHING!!!

THE POLICE ARE NOT HERE TO CREATE DISORDER, THE POLICE ARE HERE TO PRESERVE DISORDER! *

AS IT TURNS OUT, WE DIDN'T PLAY!

THERE'S HUNDREDS OF COPS ON EVERY CORNER-BEATING UP SCORES OF PEACEFUL PROTESTERS!

END THE WAR

(* ACTUAL QUOTE FROM CHICAGO'S MAYOR DALEY)

1969

NIXON TAKES OFFICE, THE WAR CONTINUES, AND THE UTOPIAN HIPPIE MOVEMENT BEGINS TO COLLAPSE; THE YOUTH REVOLUTION NEVER MADE ENOUGH REAL CONTACT WITH MIDDLE AMERICA AND THE WORKING CLASS. THINGS BEGIN TO DEPRESS POLITICALLY.

THE FUGS ARE PROBABLY NEEDED MORE THAN EVER, BUT AFTER SIX LPs ED ENDS THE BAND- HE'S BEEN THE LEADER AND ORGANIZER AND HE'S WORN OUT.

OUR LAST SHOW IS IN PENNSYLVANIA, IN FEBRUARY OF 1969, WITH THE GRATEFUL DEAD AND THE VELVET UNDERGROUND.

CINEMA SATAN'S SADISTS RATED XXX

WOO 3 DAYS OF LOVE

WOMYN'S LIB

ED MOVES TO WOODSTOCK AND BECOMES THE ACCLAIMED AUTHOR OF "THE FAMILY" (ABOUT CHARLES MANSON) AND "TALES OF BEATNIK GLORY."

192

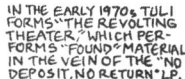

IN THE EARLY 1970s TULI FORMS "THE REVOLTING THEATER," WHICH PERFORMS "FOUND" MATERIAL IN THE VEIN OF THE "NO DEPOSIT, NO RETURN" LP.

THE 70's— A FUG-LESS DECADE. I GET MARRIED, HAVE KIDS.

I ALSO START PUBLISHING MY "MOCKINGBIRD" PARODIES, WITH POLITICAL LYRICS I WRITE TO THE TUNES OF POPULAR SONGS. "PARASONGS" ARE AN OLD TRADITION, GOING BACK TO JOE HILL AND WAY BEFORE THAT.

♪ BECAUSE THE STATE IS RUN BY FUCKERS... ♪

LISTEN TO THE MOCKINGBIRD
Satiric Songs to Tunes You Know
3rd Edition
With Over 25 New Songs
BY TULI KUPFERBERG

(*SUNG TO THE TUNE OF "BECAUSE THE NIGHT BELONGS TO LOVERS.")

1984

ED AND I RE-FORM THE FUGS, WITH NEW MEMBERS STEVE TAYLOR, COBY BATTY, AND SCOTT PETITO!

IT ACTUALLY BECOMES THE FUGS' LONGEST-LIVED LINE-UP, CONTINUING TO DO OCCASIONAL ALBUMS AND SHOWS INTO THE 21ST CENTURY.

INDEPENDENT-ROCK ICON KRAMER IS BRIEFLY A MEMBER TOO.

1989: KRAMER PRODUCES THE ALBUM "TULI & FRIENDS," AND RELEASES IT ON HIS INDEPENDENT NEW YORK LABEL SHIMMY DISC.

GUEST VOCALIST ALLEN GINSBERG SINGS TULI'S SONG "GO FUCK YOURSELF WITH YOUR ATOM BOMB."

IN THE 1980s TULI ALSO BEGINS A CAREER AS A CARTOONIST!

GREAT MOMENTS IN THE HISTORY OF THE LEFT

KARL— WHEN THE FUCK ARE YOU GONNA GET A JOB

2000: AUTONOMEDIA PUBLISHES "TEACH YOURSELF FUCKING," A WONDERFUL COLLECTION OF TULI'S CARTOONS & COLLAGES.

WHEN I HEAR THE WORD 'CULTURE' I REACH FOR MY GUN...

WHEN I HEAR THE WORD 'GUN' I REACH FOR MY CULTURE.

2007

I'M 84 NOW, STILL POLITICALLY ACTIVE AND STILL LIVING IN SOHO WITH SYLVIA TOPP.

WITH THELMA BLITZ I DO A HOMEMADE NY PUBLIC ACCESS TV SHOW CALLED "REVOLTING NEWS"...

I'M DRAWING, WRITING, AND COLLECTING "PARASONGS" FOR FUTURE EDITIONS OF THE MOCKINGBIRD.

THE MOST RECENT FUGS RELEASES ARE THE AMAZING 2003 "FUGS FINAL CD PART I" AND "THE BEST OF THE FUGS 1984-2004," A COMPILATION SHOWCASING LIVE AND STUDIO RECORDINGS FROM THE RE-FORMED FUGS INCLUDING MODERN FUGS CLASSICS SUCH AS "DREAMS OF SEXUAL PERFECTION" AND "TRY TO BE JOYFUL." A FORTHCOMING 4-CD FUGS BOX SET WILL INCLUDE BRAND-NEW MATERIAL AND PREVIOUSLY UNRELEASED EARLY REEL-TO-REEL SONGS. SEE WWW.THEFUGS.COM FOR MORE ABOUT EVERYTHING.

About Our Artists and Writers

Joyce Brabner is a writer of political comics and sometime collaborator with her husband, Harvey Pekar, and has appeared as a character in many of his *American Splendor* stories. Brabner has also worked with many of independent comics' highest-profile writers and artists in projects including *Real War Stories*, the Harvey Award–winning graphic novel *Our Cancer Year*, and Jason Rodriguez's "Postcards" series.

Paul Buhle, a senior lecturer at Brown University, has written or edited thirty-five books but is proudest of his comic art series, of which this volume is a part.

Gary Dumm, a lifelong Cleveland resident, has worked with Harvey Pekar on *American Splendor* since Pekar's self-publishing began thirty years ago. He drew the bulk of *Students for a Democratic Society: A Graphic History*. His work has been exhibited internationally, and his art has appeared in *Entertainment Weekly*, *The New York Times*, and *Le Monde*, among other places. He contends that he will continue drawing comics and cartoons until they pry his weapon of choice (pencil, pen, brush, or marker) from his cold, dead hand.

Mary Fleener has had a varied career in underground comics, illustration, painting, and ceramics. She's best known for her book, *Life of the Party*. She currently lives in Encinitas, California, with her husband, Paul Therrio. They also play music and have a band called the Wigbillies.

Jay Kinney is an author, editor, and former underground cartoonist. A member, along with Skip Williamson, Jay Lynch, and R. Crumb, of the original *Bijou Funnies* crew, Kinney also edited the romance comic satire *Young Lust* throughout the 1970s with Bill Griffith. He later founded the political comic *Anarchy Comics*, which was published through the early 1980s. He has also written two books and published *Gnosis Magazine* (1985–1999), all focused on aspects of Western esoteric traditions.

In 1979 *Peter Kuper* cofounded the political graphics magazine *World War 3 Illustrated*. He is also an art director of INX, a political illustration group syndicated through the web at inxart.com. Peter has done covers for *Time* and *Newsweek* as well as *Mad*, where he has been writing and drawing "SPY vs. SPY" every month since 1997. He has written and illustrated dozens of books, including *Sticks and Stones*, which won the New York Society of Illustrators gold medal, and his autobiography, *Stop Forgetting to Remember*. He has done adaptations of Franz Kafka's work, including *The Metamorphosis*, and Upton Sinclair's *The Jungle*. A compilation of his sketchbooks and writing about the experience of living in Mexico for the last two years, *Diario de Oaxaca*, has just been released. More of his work can be seen at www.peterkuper.com.

Jeffrey Lewis was born on roughly the same day that *Giant Size X-Men #1* came out in November 1975. Raised by loving beatnik parents on New York's Lower East Side and educated by the public school system, he is no longer in mint condition but has nevertheless accrued slightly in value. Currently he has a body that resides in Brooklyn when not on tour, albums of songs released on the Rough Trade label, and comics in various publications floating around the margins of western civilization, including the magazines *World War 3 Illustrated*, his own occasional comic *Foof*, and the history volume *Wobblies! A Graphic History of the Industrial Workers of the World*. Visit www.thejeffreylewissite.com.

Summer McClinton is a modern-day beatnik chick living and working in New York City. Her comic book credits include *Thread Comics*, *Students for a Democratic Society: A Graphic History*, and Harvey Pekar's *Huntington W. V., On the Fly*. She is currently open to sudden revelation.

Jerome Neukirch is a persnickety perfectionist and a hopeless procrastinator. He has never turned anything in on time—including this bio. His main claim to fame is having worked with Harvey Pekar previously, and that art was late too. When not trying to draw, Jerome is an unimportant functionary in academia and an aspiring writer. He has two adoring cats who support his work and have always shown a sustained interest in the production process. He is not a beatnik, but does have a beard and several black turtlenecks.

Harvey Pekar, first made famous by appearances on *Late Night with David Letterman* and then by the award-winning 2003 film *American Splendor,* began a self-published comic by that name in 1976. His latest script work includes *Students for a Democratic Society: A Graphic History*, *Macedonia*, and the forthcoming adaptation of Studs Terkel's *Working*.

Nancy Joyce Peters is an author and publisher and co-owner with Lawrence Ferlinghetti of the City Lights Bookstore.

Ed Piskor resides in Pittsburgh, where he draws comics constantly, all the while avoiding most other obligations that life may bring. Harvey Pekar wrote some books that Ed got to draw. Ed's been doing his own comics lately, such as the serialized graphic novel *Wizzywig*.

Trina Robbins, one of the founding figures of underground comix and the leading scholar of women comic and cartoon artists in the United States, has been writing comics, books, and graphic novels for more than thirty years. She lives in a dusty 105-year-old house in San Francisco with her books, shoes, and cats.

Penelope Rosemont, longtime surrealist and Chicago cultural/political activist, has written or edited several books, including the memoir *Dreams & Everyday Life* and the important collection *Surrealist Women: An International Anthology*.

Nick Thorkelson's comics and cartoons include *The Underhanded History of the USA* (with Jim O'Brien), the "Econotoons" and "Comic Strip of Neoliberalism" features in *Dollars & Sense* magazine, and a regular series of cartoons on local politics for *The Boston Globe*. He contributed to *Wobblies! A Graphic History of the Industrial Workers of the World* and *Students for a Democratic Society: A Graphic History*.

Native Oregonian *Anne Timmons* has teamed up with comics legend *Trina Robbins* on several projects, including illustrated biographies of Hedy Lamarr and Florence Nightingale, an adaptation of Jane Austen's *Northanger Abbey* in Graphic Classics volume 14, and the award-winning *GoGirl!* Currently they are creating a full-color adaptation of *Little Women* for Graphic Classics. Anne's art for a biography of primatologist Birute Galdikas was included in the Eisner-nominated *Dignifying Science*. Anne also contributed artwork for the upcoming graphic adaptation of Studs Terkel's *Working*.

Lance Tooks has been drawing all his life. A former assistant editor at Marvel Comics, his artwork has since appeared in more than a hundred television commercials, films, and music videos. In addition to self-publishing comic works, his comics have appeared in *Zuzu*, *Shade*, *Vibe*, *Girltalk*, *World War 3 Illustrated*, Spike Lee's *Floaters*, and the Italian magazine *Lupo Alberto*. He also illustrated *The Black Panthers for Beginners*, written by Herb Boyd, and contributed to a Hurricane Katrina benefit comic as well as to the Graphic Classics line of adaptations. He recently completed his first graphic novel and a four-volume series entitled *Lucifer's Garden of Verses*. Lance Tooks lives in New York and Madrid. He merely exists everywhere else.

Acknowledgments

Long-distance thanks for this volume go to people who kept the lamps burning in the story of the literary rebels, and made the case personally to the editor of this volume (among many others): Lawrence Ferlinghetti, Tuli Kupferberg, Diane di Prima, Franklin Rosemont, the late Philip Lamantia, the late Robert Creeley, the late Allen Ginsberg, and the late d.a. levy. And to everyone who has ever worked at City Lights Press and Bookstore, the real home of the Beats and their legacy. Closer to the present, gratitude goes to Christine Bunting of the University of California, Santa Cruz, the librarian who assisted us in permissions to quote Kenneth Patchen; to Larry Keenan, whose photography of City Lights Bookstore provided inspiration for Jay Kinney; to Ed Sanders, who kindly granted us permission to use the lyrics of the Fugs; to an unfailing advocate of Gary Snyder, my longtime collaborator Dave Wagner; to the singularly important scholar of City Lights, James Gatewood; and finally to Hill and Wang's publisher, Thomas LeBien, and his assistant, Elizabeth Maples, for all their efforts.